UNDERSTANDING
SOCIALISM

Madeleine Templeton

"Aunt Kitty"

authorHOUSE®

AuthorHouse™
1663 Liberty Drive
Bloomington, IN 47403
www.authorhouse.com
Phone: 833-262-8899

Published by AuthorHouse 09/15/2022

ISBN: 978-1-6655-6750-3 (sc)
ISBN: 978-1-6655-6749-7 (hc)
ISBN: 978-1-6655-6751-0 (e)

Library of Congress Control Number: 2022914474

Print information available on the last page.

Any people depicted in stock imagery provided by Getty Images are models, and such images are being used for illustrative purposes only. Certain stock imagery © Getty Images.

This book is printed on acid-free paper.

CONTENTS

DEDICATION

I dedicate this book to my niece, Reagan, who is the sole inspiration for this work and its completion. I love you very much!

Acknowledgements

Linda M. Wright- Editor
Adrian Zegarra – A-Z Computer Services
AuthorHouse Publishing

A book to help save America from a socialist future
A profile of America in 2022
How to keep America America

PREFACE

The story behind the genesis of this pamphlet is an interesting one:

It was the summer of 2019. I was vacationing with my family at their farm in Virginia. My 15-year-old niece was attending her annual summer camp for two weeks. Traditionally, our family likes to take this opportunity to vacation, get away, relax, and enjoy some togetherness and family time. It was one warm evening; the sunshine was spilling in the backroom, and we were setting the table for dinner. My Dad was watching his usual evening news on the television. Politics came up as we were setting the table, and I asked my niece, Reagan, "Do you know what Socialism is?" And she responded: "I've heard the word, but I do not know what it means". I thought, wow, such a loaded question to ask a teenager.

I was not prepared to tell her what it was! It was too much to explain to her in words, what it meant. Usually, I am better at writing my thoughts than speaking them. I have never been able to discuss politics cleverly enough to persuade my listener. My Dad has this talent, he is a very good political talker, and persuader, but it took me over 40 years of my life to understand what he was really talking about...

After I came home from our summer vacation I thought: "If I could not tell Reagan what Socialism is, then maybe I could explain it in writing?" I got to work on my computer. I had the rough outline already in my head, and I popped on and started the necessary research. I had majored in History at college, and I had the necessary "know how" to come up with this paper. I drafted my first copy by November 17th, 2019, right on time for Thanksgiving!

After many revisions, updates, and redo's I thought: *"If my niece can benefit from this, so could many teens, and young students, either in high school, or college!"* This is the challenging part, it is my dream to be able to reach students and the youth of America, in a pertinent and powerful way in order for them to understand that they do not live in the worst place in the world, quite the opposite! It is my hope to explain these differing economic philosophies in the simplest way possible. If you don't know a word, look it up on your phone. Enjoy your reading and remember to get out to vote!

This is a work rooted in love. Love for my country, and love for the youth in America, and especially to my niece. Truly yours, from your Aunt Kitty.

"I am not bound to win, but I am bound to be true. I am not bound to success, but I am bound to live up to what light I have inside me."

-Abraham Lincoln

What is Socialism?
Introduction to
Karl Marx

<u>DEFINITION:</u>

So·cial·ism
/ˈsōSHəˌlizəm/

<u>Noun:</u>

A way of organizing a society in which major industries are owned and controlled by the government rather than by individual people and companies

  a) a system of society or group living in which there is no private property
  b) a system or condition of society in which the means of production is owned and controlled by the state

A stage of society in Marxist theory transitional between Capitalism and Communism

Similar:

leftism	militancy
Fabianism	progressivism
syndicalism	social democracy
consumer socialism	laborism
utopian socialism	Marxism
welfarism	Leninism
communism	Marxism–Leninism
Bolshevism	neo-Marxism
radicalism	Trotskyism
Maoism	

Opposite:

Conservatism

Antonyms:

Freedom	liberty
Democracy	Individual Liberty
self-governance	human rights
Republic	free world
free enterprise	rule of law
capitalism	

According to *Oxford Dictionaries* Socialism is: *"A political and economic theory of social organization which advocates that the means of production, distribution, and exchange should be owned or regulated by the community as a whole."*

"Policy or practice based on the political and economic theory of socialism. (In Marxist theory) a transitional social state between the overthrow of capitalism and the realization of Communism."

KARL MARX (1818-1883) was a German philosopher, author, social theorist, and an Economist. He is famous for his theories about capitalism and communism. He is called the Father of Marxism and a Father of Socialism and Father of Communism.

Karl Marx, in full **Karl Heinrich Marx,** (born May 5, 1818, Trier, Rhine province, Prussia [Germany]—died March 14th, 1883, London, England), revolutionary, sociologist, historian, and economist. He published (with Friedrich Engels) *Manifest der Kommunistishen Partei* (1848), commonly known as *The Communist Manifesto,* the most celebrated pamphlet in the history of the socialist movement.

He also was the author of the movement's most important book, *Das Kapital* (Capital). These writing and others by Marx and Engels form the basis of the body of thought and belief know as Marxism.

Socialism is a step in becoming a Communist State- **Read**: *"The Communist Manifesto"* to learn more, it will explain the steps involved to reach Communism from Capitalism: by **Karl Marx and Friedrich Engles**. Communism is Marx's idea of a "Utopian" State (Study Russian History), but once the revolution then what?

Karl Marx Is best remembered for advocating socialism, particularly the brand that would take his name. As the father of Marxism, Marx predicted that capitalistic societies, ruled by a "dictatorship of the bourgeoise" would eventually give way via class struggle to a "dictatorship of the proletariat", and eventually to a more stateless (classless) form of communism.

This would occur through revolution. *"See equality of wages as the goal of social revolution... and that alienation of the proletariat (workers) and its potential as a revolutionary force."* (Marx)

Marx also perceived that Religion was an oppressor of the state. In what Marx believed is a perfect political and economic state is in fact the emergence of communism from an overthrown capitalist society. In a communist state there is no Religion. He went on to say Religion is "the opiate of the people." In Marx's vision of the United States, he asserts that people are not "freed from religion; he received freedom of religion."

The immediate aftermath of the revolution, they propose (Marx and Hegel) will see a "Dictatorship of the proletariat" in which laboring class seizes control of the means of production to which it was previously subjected. In order to do so, the proletariat also takes control of the state, and uses this control to expropriate private property in order to make it the common property of all:

Confiscation of property
Centralization of all assets and credits (money)
Centralization of the means of communication (news)
and transport (transportation)

"With these measure in place, in the hands of the state, it will sweep away the conditions for the existence of class antagonism. And the proletariat will thereby abolish its own supremacy as a class." (Marx)

Marx, the philosopher, often reflected on the difference between "what is" and "what ought to be". In living through the period of the European Age of Romanticism, Marx believed in "the ideals of the imagination over the measurable facts of observed reality, and that objects would only obtain reality in so far as they are perceived in the conscious mind."

Thereby stating that this philosophy, is in fact theoretical, and that Marx's theories had up to this point (his death) had not been tested.

Lord Acton wrote a letter to Bishop Mandell in 1887 where Acton states: *"Power tends to corrupt, and absolute power corrupts absolutely".* Marx died in 1883, five years before the emergence of this statement. His whole life's work could possibly be contradicted with this argument.

In these next pages, I will site four examples of how dictators have used Marx's theories to gain total control in their countries and their terrible outcomes.

Four examples of countries that had suffered or are suffering from Socialism and their Dictators:

Russia- (USSR) The Soviet Union- Lenin, Stalin, and now Putin
China- Mao Zedong, and the Chinese Communist Party (CCP)
Nazi Germany- Adolf Hitler
Venezuela- Nicolás Maduro

*I am not going in depth about CUBA in this paper, but Cuba has had a socialist political system since 1959 based on the "one state-one party" principle. Cuba is constitutionally defined as a Marxist-Leninist socialist state guided in part by the political ideas of Karl Marx and headed by Fidel Castro who died in 2016.

#1: Russia

USSR = Union of Soviet Socialist Republic = (Soviet Union)

The Soviet Union was a former northern Eurasian empire (1917/22-1991) stretching from the Baltic and Black seas to the Pacific Ocean and, in its final years, consisting of **15 Soviet Socialist Republics.**

In post-revolutionary Russia, the Union of Soviet Socialist Republics (USSR) is established, comprising a confederation of Russia, Belorussia, Ukraine, and the Transcaucasian Federation (divided in 1946 into the Georgian, Azerbaijan and Armenian republics). Also known as the Soviet Union, the new communist state was the successor to the Russian Empire and the first country in the world to be based on Marxist socialism.

During the Russian Revolution of 1917 and subsequent three-year Russian Civil War, the Bolshevik Party under Vladimir Lenin dominated the *soviet* forces, a coalition of workers' and soldiers' committees that called for the establishment of a socialist state in the former Russian Empire. In the USSR, all levels of government were controlled by the Communist Party, and the party's politburo, with its increasingly powerful general secretary, effectively ruled the country.

Soviet industry was owned and managed by the state, and agricultural land was divided into state-run collective farms.

Vladimir Lenin, also called **Vladimir Ilich Lenin**, original **name Vladimir Ilich Ulyanov**, (born April 10 [April 22, New Style], 1870, Simbirsk, Russia—died January 21, 1924, Gorki [later Gorki Leninskiye] near Moscow), founder of the Russian Communist Party (Bolsheviks), inspirer and leader of the Bolshevik Revolution (1917), and the architect, builder, and first head (1917-24) of the Soviet state. He was the founder of the organization known as Comintern (Communist International) and the posthumous source of "Leninism", the doctrine codified and conjoined with Karl Marx's works by Lenin's successors to form Marxism-Leninism, which became the Communist worldview.

Bolsheviks armed with guns rode in a truck in Vladivostok, Russia, in 1920. Led by Vladimir Lenin, the left-wing Bolshevik regime sought to silence its enemies through a state-sanctioned policy of mass killings and detainments known as the Red Terror.

The Red Terror was a Bolshevik- ordered campaign of intimidation, arrests, violence, and executions. It began in mid-1918 following an assassination attempt of Vladimir Lenin and was carried out chiefly by the Cheka, the Bolshevik secret police. The Red Terror was a determined campaign that sought to eliminate opposition, political dissent, and threats to Bolshevik power.

Joseph Stalin- Born: December 5th, 1878, December 18th, 1878, Gori Georgia; died March 5th, 1953 (aged 74) Moscow

1901
The Revolutionary Bandit

While working as a clerk at the Meteorological Observatory, Joseph Stalin carries on with his revolutionary activities, organizing strikes and protests.

His activities become known to the Tsarist secret police, and he is forced to go underground. He joins the Bolshevik party and conducts guerrilla warfare for the first time in the 1905 Russian Revolution. His first meeting with Lenin, the Bolshevik leader, is at a party conference in Finland. Lenin is impressed by this 'ruthless underground operator'. In 1907 Joseph steals 250,000 rubles (approximately $3.4m in US dollars) in a bank robbery in Tiflis to help fund the cause.

After Lenin's death in 1924, Stalin begins ruthlessly promoting himself as his political heir.

1929
Stalin Promotes Himself to Dictator

Many in the party expected Red Army leader Leon Trotsky to be Lenin's natural successor, but his ideas are too idealistic for the majority of the Communist Party. Stalin, however, develops his own nationalistic brand of Marxism— "Socialism for One Country" – concentrating on strengthening the Soviet Union rather than world revolution. When Trotsky criticizes his plans, Stalin has him exiled, and then killed in

Mexico. Stalin's ideas are popular with the party and by the late 1920's he becomes dictator of the Soviet Union.

March 25th, (March 12, Old Style), 1917, Stalin resumed editorship of *Pravda* ("*The Truth*"- Soviet newspaper), which is still the Russian run newspaper today.

Naimark, author of the controversial new book *Stalin's Genocides*, argues that we need a much broader definition of genocide, one that includes nations killing social classes and political groups. His case in point: Stalin.

The book's title is plural for a reason: He argues that Soviet elimination of a social class, the kulaks (who were higher-income farmers), and the subsequent killer famine among all Ukrainian peasants- as well as the notorious 1937 order No. 00447 that called for the mass execution and exile of "socially harmful elements" as "enemies of the people" – were, in fact, genocide.

"I make the argument that these matters shouldn't be seen as discrete episodes, but seen together," said Naimark, the Robert and Florence McDonnell Professor of Eastern European Studies and a respected authority on the Soviet regime, *"It's a horrific case of genocide – the purposeful elimination of all or part of a social group, a political group."*

Stalin had nearly a million of his own citizens executed, beginning in the 1930s. Millions more fell victim to forced labor, deportation, famine, massacres, and detention and interrogation by Stalin's henchmen.

1934-39
Stalin's Great Terror

Stalin promotes an image of himself as a great benevolent leader and hero of the Soviet Union. Yet he is increasingly paranoid and purges the Communist party and Army of anyone who might oppose him. Ninety three of the 139 Central Committee members are killed and 81 of the 103 generals and admirals are executed (in Stalin's **Great Purge**). The secret police strictly enforce Stalinism and people are encouraged to inform on one another. Three million people are accused of opposing Communism and sent to the gulag, a system of labor camps in Siberia. Around 750,000 people are summarily killed.

If one includes the combatant deaths, and the deaths due to war-related famine and disease, the number shoot up astronomically. The Soviet Union suffered upward of 8 million combatant deaths (in WWII) and many more due to famine and disease—**perhaps about 20 million.**

Mass killing is still the way a lot of governments do business. In past few decades have seen terrifying examples [of this] in Rwanda, Cambodia, Darfur, Bosnia.

Russia Today:

Vladimir Putin – President of Russia since 2012

Now Russia is involved in a war with Ukraine over power and territory. Putin claims Ukraine is still a part of Russia and has attacked Ukraine, a sovereign nation, with military force while weakening Russia's economy with a full-fledged war. Russia's economy ranks 11th in the world, and it's roughly one-fourteenth of the size of the United States economy, the world's biggest.

To justify invading Ukraine, Vladimir Putin has painted Russia as a hegemonic power re-asserting its rightful claim to imperial greatness. Yet even before the invasion, Russia's economic capabilities were hardly capable of sustaining an empire.

Now with foreign sanctions presiding over a plummeting Russian ruble, Russia's economic standing has fallen further still. If measure at today's exchange rates, Russia's economy would be the 22nd largest in the world, with a gross domestic product (GDP) not much larger than the state of Ohio's.

"[Putin] *said it before the war, that Ukraine is not a nation that Ukrainians do not exist, that this land belongs to him, to Russia, he confuses a little bit the states, the government and himself, but he really is sure that Ukraine as a country is just a part of Russia, and the Ukrainian people, if you call yourself Ukrainian that means you are neither here, so that means you should be eliminated. He clearly stated before the war he will just come here and try to kill as many people as possible, those who will be left will be put into secret prisons. I mean he put his own people for 15 years into the prisons simply if they state and go out on the streets saying, "no war", here they will be put into prisons for 15 years. Imagine if we are defeated?*

It's clear what he wants to do, it is clear we must not let him do this, together with the help of you and others, we are human beings we are authentic for the free world and these atrocities in the 21ˢᵗ Century, shouldn't happen, this is nonsense. Putin needs to be stopped, he is now a criminal, he is not a politician anymore, it's now official before it was just me and children saying this, but now it is high ranking politicians that confess he is a criminal, he is a terrorist, he needs to be stopped by force because force is the only language he understands, but I do not trust him at all because he promised many times that he will not kill civilians, but they are shooting in the communitarian corridors people, children are being targeted.

They are killed, children are losing their limbs, their lives, it's just awful I do not understand how we can seriously discuss all of this…" (Elana -Ukrainian Mom)

Putin is an authoritarian dictator a *"soviet style KGB cold blooded killer."* (Koffler) He uses the only Russian newspaper *PRAVDA,* meaning "truth," to push his justification of the war, and tell the people of Russia that things are all ok, when they are not: *"It is fake news, it's not the truth, it is what the government wants you to believe…"* (a Russian teen)

"This is suspected to be Vladimir Putin's 700-million-dollar yacht it is currently moored in Italy. Putin's people are suffering under sanctions, he's slaughtering Ukrainian citizens. At least 15,000 of his own citizens are in jails right now and were getting reports of torture and all kinds of things to people in custody for speaking out against the war." (Faulkner)

Tyrus jests: *"His yacht game is strong…'700 million dollars, that's almost a billion of the people's money! 'The people's boat' …I wonder how this works out, is there a waiting list? Does everyone get a turn, do you book a family? Graduations? Proms?"* (Tyrus) No. It's Putin's boat. Nobody enjoys this 700-million-dollar yacht but Putin.

"This is authoritarianism, this is a dictatorship, this is communism, this is socialism, the ruling elite play by their own rules and enrich themselves on the backs of regular people and then they go make those regular people those "peasants" go fight wars in foreign lands because of their egos or ambitions

of re-capturing the past. This is the worst of human nature laid to bare in Vladimir Putin." (Hegseth)

#2: China

In the case of China, socialism is not only about equality. It is supposed to take the country towards an ultimate goal – Communism.

Communism, according to German philosopher Karl Marx, is a society without class divisions… or any government. In that perfect world, everyone would be voluntarily working for the public, and at the same time, receiving whatever they needed from publicly owned institutions.

Between the abolition of capitalism and the establishment of full Communism, Marx said there would be a transitional period when the working class rules the bourgeoisie (socialism). The Chinese Communist Party was established in 1921 for that purpose. Until now, officials still maintain the idea of building a socialist society and, one day, reaching the goal of Communism.

On October 1, 1949, Chinese Communist leader Mao Zedong declared the creation of the People's Republic of China (PRC). The announcement ended the costly full- scale civil war between the Chinese Communist Party (CCP) and the Nationalist Party, or Kuomintang (KMT), led by Chen Kai Check, which broke out immediately following World War II and had been preceded by on and off conflict between the two sides since the 1920's.

The creation of the PRC (People's Republic of China) also completed the long process of governmental upheaval in China begun by the Chinese Revolution or 1911. The "fall" of mainland China to communism in 1949 led the United States to suspend diplomatic ties with the PRC for decades.

When the People's Republic was founded in 1949, China embraced the Marxist-Leninist style of socialism wholeheartedly. During the reforms of the 1950s, rural China was divided into numerous "communes:" big, collective farms owned by the state.

Urban China had work units. Private property was abolished.

Mao Zedong, founder of the People's Republic of China, qualifies as the greatest mass murderer in world history, according to an expert who had unprecedented access to official Communist Party archives.

Speaking at *The Independent* Woodstock Literary Festival, Frank Dikötter, a Hong Kong-based historian, said he found that during the time that Mao was enforcing the Great Leap Forward in 1958, in an effort to catch up with the economy of the Western world, he was responsible for overseeing *"one of the worst catastrophes the world has ever known"*.

Mr. Dikötter, who is the only author to have delved into the Chinese archives since they were opened four years ago. He argued that this devastating period of history-which until now has remained hidden-has international resonance. *"It ranks alongside the gulags and the Holocaust as one of the three greatest events in the 20th Century... It was like [the Cambodian communist dictator] Pol Pot's genocide multiplied 20 times over"* he said.

Mao's Great Leap Forward 'Killed 45 million in four years.

Between 1958 and 1962, a war raged between the peasants and the state; it was a period when a third of all homes were destroyed to produce fertilizer and when the nation descended into famine and starvation, Mr. Dittoker said.

His book, **"Mao's Great Famine: The Story of China's Most Devastating Catastrophe"**, reveals that while this is a part of history that has been "quite forgotten" in the official memory of the People's Republic of China, there was a "staggering degree of violence" that was, remarkable, carefully catalogued in Public Security Bureau reports, which featured among the provincial archives he studied. In them, he found that the member of the rural farming communities was seen by the Party mere's as "digits" or a faceless workforce. For those committed any acts of disobedience, however minor, the punishments were huge.

State retribution for tiny thefts, such as stealing a potato, even by a child, would include being tied up and thrown into a pond; parents were forced to bury their children alive or were doused in excrement and urine, others were set alight, or had a nose or ear cut off.

One record show how a man was branded with hot metal. People were forced to work naked in the middle of winter; 80 percent of all the villagers in one region of a quarter of a million Chinese were banned from the official canteen because they were too old or ill to be effective workers, so they were deliberately starved to death.

Mr. Dikötter said that he was once again examining the Party's archives for his next book, The Tragedy of Liberation, which will deal with the bloody advent of Communism in China from 1944 to 1957.

He said the archives were already illuminating the extent of the atrocities of the period; one piece of evidence revealed that 13,000 political opponents of the new regime were killed in one region alone, in just three weeks. *We know the outline of what went on, but I will be looking into precisely what happened in this period, how it happened, and the human experience behind the history,* he said.

Mr. Dikötter, who teaches at the University of Hong Kong, said while it was difficult for any historian in China to write books that are critical of Mao, he felt he could not collude with the "conspiracy of silence" in what the Chinese rural community had suffered in recent history.

In this communist state, Mao Zedong initiated absolute power and centralized government. To this day, China remains a communist state, and there is no Religion. It had *almost* fulfilled its steps to what Marx's idea of a perfect utopian state should be, except the winners of this revolution (The Communist Party) did not abolish its own supremacy as a class, and The Communist Party (CCP) never relinquished its control. The People's Republic of China's current government is controlled by the Chinese Communist Party led by Xi Jing Ping. Therein lies the caveat with Karl Marx's theory; the party that wins the proletariat socialist revolution historically has NEVER turned over their power to back the people, thus leaving the power in the hands of the Communist Party, or the newly formed Communist state.

Communist China Today:

Multiple media and NGOs (Non-Government Organizations) estimated that since April 2017, the government detained at least 800,000 and up to possibly more than 2 million Uighurs (pronounced wee-gars), ethnic Kazakhs, and members of other Muslim groups, mostly Chinese citizens, in specially built or converted detention facilities in Xinjiang and subjected them to forced disappearance, torture, physical abuse, and prolonged detention without trial because of their religion and ethnicity....Religious groups reported deaths in or shortly after detentions, disappearances, and arrests and stated authorities tortured Tibetan Buddhists, Christians, and members of Falun Gong. The Church of Almighty God reported authorities subjected hundreds of their members to 'torture of forced indoctrination'. *"The first thing that authoritarians try to do is to delegitimize and ban Religion because it is an existential threat against the state."* (Campos- Duffy)

In today's China, there are still many atrocities playing out: humanitarian ethics, organ harvesting, suppression of freedom in Hong Kong, torture of political opponents, no ability to worship any Religion, an economy that relies on stolen technologies and intellectual properties and unequal and unreciprocated trade to USA and the world, and government control. *"China has been destabilizing our economy for decades, destroying our working class, and stealing our intellectual properties"* (Hilton).

On February 1st, 2022, Enes Kanter Freedom advised American athletes going to China to compete in the 2022 Olympics in Beijing that: *"they need to understand the CCP does not represent all of the big core values of excellence of respect of friendship and the whole world knows now they are a brutal dictatorship, and they need to understand they engage in censorship, they track our freedoms, they do not respect human rights."* (Freedom).

China is the biggest global threat to the United States.

#3: Nazi Germany

Nazi Party
Political party, Germany
NSDAP= **National Socialist German Workers Party**= Nazi Party

Nationalsozialistische Deutsche Arbeiterpartei (NSDAP), political party of the mass movement know as **National Socialism**. Under, the leadership of Adolf Hitler, the **Nazi** Party came to power in Germany in 1933 and governed by totalitarian methods until 1945.

The Nazi Party was founded as the German Workers' Party by Anton Drexler, a Munich locksmith, in 1919. Hitler attended one of its meetings that year, and before long his energy and oratorical skills would enable him to take over the party, which was renamed National Socialist German Workers' Party in 1920. That year Hitler also formulated a 25-point program that became the permanent basis for the party. The program called for German abandonment of the Treaty of Versailles and for the expansion of German territory. These appeals for national aggrandizement were accompanied by a strident anti-Semitic rhetoric. The party's socialist orientation was basically a demagogic gambit designed to attract support from the working class. By 1921 Hitler had ousted the party's other leaders and taken over.

In 1925, Adolf Hitler wrote in *Mein Kampf*, *"Everything we admire on this earth today—science and art, technology, and inventions—is only the creative product of a few peoples and originally perhaps one race [the "Aryans"]. On them depends on the existence of this whole culture. If they perish, the beauty of this earth will sink into the grave with them."* From the start, the Nazis were determined to ensure the strength and purity of the "Aryan" race. They believed, according to historian Richard Evans, that *"the strong and the racially pure had to be encouraged to have more children, the weak and the racially impure had to be neutralized by one means or another."*

However, it was the effects of the Great Depression in Germany that brought the Nazi Party to its first real nationwide importance. The rapid rise in unemployment in 1929—30 provided millions of jobless and dissatisfied voters whom the Nazi Party exploited to its advantage.

From 1929 to 1932 the party vastly increased its membership and voting strength; its vote in election to the Reichstag (the German Parliament) increased from 800, 000 votes in 1928 to about 14,000,000 votes in July 1932, and it thus emerged as the largest voting bloc in the Reichstag, with 230 members (38 percent of the total vote). By then big-business circles had begun to finance the Nazi electoral campaigns and swelling bands of SA toughs increasingly dominated the street fighting with the communists that accompanied such campaigns.

When unemployment began to drop in Germany in late 1932, the Nazi Party's vote also dropped, to about 12,000,000 (33 percent of the vote) in the November 1932 elections.

Nevertheless, Hitler's shrewd maneuvering behind the scenes prompted the president of the German republic, Paul von Hindenburg, to name him chancellor on January 30, 1933. Hitler used the powers of his office to solidify the Nazis' position in the government during the following months. The elections of March 5, 1933—precipitated by the burning of the Reichstag (the German Parliament) building only days earlier—gave the Nazi Party 44 percent of the votes, and further unscrupulous tactics on Hitler's part turned the voting balance in the Reichstag in the Nazis' favor. On March 23, 1933, the Reichstag passed the Enabling Act, which "enabled" Hitler's government to issue decrees independently of the Reichstag and the presidency; Hitler in effect assumed dictatorial powers.

On July 14, 1933, Hitler's government declared the Nazi Party to be the only political party in Germany. On the death of Hindenburg in 1934 Hitler took the titles of Führer ("Leader"), chancellor, and commander in chief of the army, and he remained leader of the Nazi Party as well. Nazi Party membership became mandatory for all higher civil servants and bureaucrats, and the gauleiters became powerful figures in the state governments. Hitler crushed the Nazi Party's left, or social-oriented, wing in 1934, executing Ernst Röhm and other rebellious SA leaders on what would become known as the "Night of the Long Knives". Thereafter, Hitler's word was the supreme and undisputed command in the party. Its vast and complex hierarchy was structured like a pyramid, with party-controlled mass organizations for youth, women, workers, and other groups at the bottom, party members and officials in the middle, and Hitler and his closest associates at the top wielding undisputed authority.

The years between 1934 and 1938 were used by the party to establish virtual total control of all political, social, and cultural activities in Germany. This phase began in earnest with the death of Hindenburg on August 2, 1934. The functions of the military and government were subsumed into the party, and all troops and officials were forced to take the oath of fidelity to Hitler personally. Subordination of the broader German populace was achieved primarily through to the unification of all the police, security, and Schutzstaffel (SS) organizations under the direction of Heinrich Himmler and his chief lieutenant, Reinhard Heydrich.

A core element of the Nazi Party ideology was anti-Semitism, and Hitler used this period of consolidation to mobilize the power of the Nazi police state against Germany's Jewish citizens.

Jews were deprived of virtually all legal rights under the Nürnberg Laws of September 15 1935, and prewar state-sponsored persecution of Jews reached its climax on Kristallnacht (November 9-10, 1938) minister of Propaganda Joseph Goebbels ordered these pogroms, in which SS-directed rioters damaged or destroyed more than 1,000 synagogues and ransacked some 7,500 Jewish owned homes and businesses. Scores of Jews were killed in the violence, and tens of thousands man and boys were arrested and imprisoned in concentration camps. After Kristallnacht, the bulk of all Jewish property was confiscated, and Germany's Jews were effectively erased from public life.

When Germany started World War II, it came as the logical outcome of Hitler's plans—known to Germans since the publication of *Mein Kampf* (1926)—and of his systematic preparations since 1933. From the beginning, the Nazis did not intend to establish a new order of authoritarian and inequality for Germany alone. Therein Nazism imitated communism.

The outbreak of war also saw the full implementation of the Nazi Party's "final solutions to the Jewish question" in all areas controlled by the Third Reich. The ultimate goal of the Nazis' anti-Semitic ideology was nothing less than *Vernichtung* ("annihilation) of Europe's Jewish population. Jews in occupied territories were forced into ghettoes or systematically killed. Mass shooting by Einsatzgruppen units gave way to the industrialized murder of millions in concentration and extermination camps.

The Nazis killed victims from other groups—homosexuals, Roma, Jehovah's Witnesses, Poles, and political opponents were chief among them—but the destruction of European Jewry remained paramount in the eyes of the Third Reich. In German-occupied Europe, out of a prewar population of about 8.3 million Jews, some 6 million were killed or died in extermination camps of starvation or disease.

Six Million Jews were Murdered

The word "Holocaust," from the Greek words "holos" (whole) and "kaustos" (burned), was historically used to describe a sacrificial offering burned on an altar. Since 1945, the word has taken on a horrible new meaning: the ideological and systematic state-sponsored persecution and mass murder of millions of European Jews (as well as millions of others, including Romani people, the intellectually disabled, dissidents and homosexuals) by the German Nazi regime between 1933 and 1945.

To the anti-Semitic Nazi leader Adolf Hitler, Jews were an inferior race, an alien threat to German racial purity and community. After years of Nazi rule in Germany, during which Jews were consistently persecuted, Hitler's "final solution"—now known as the Holocaust—came to fruition under the cover of World War II, with mass killing centers constructed in the concentration camps of occupied Poland. Approximately six million Jews and some 5 million others, targeted for racial, political, ideological, and behavioral reasons, died in the Holocaust. More than one million of those who perished were children. In total **11 million people** perished Hitler's concentration camps.

As you study World History, you will learn more about Nazi Germany and Hitler in the 20th Century History of WWI and WWII. Hitler is one of the most studied and fascinated upon historical murderers.

#4: Venezuela

Nicolás Maduro – President of Venezuela, Candidate of the **United Socialist Party**

Nicolás Maduro, in full **Nicolás Maduro Moros,** (born November 23, 1962, Caracas, Venezuela), Venezuelan politician and labor leader who won the special election held in April 2013 to choose a president to serve out the remainder of the term of Pres. Hugo Chávez, who had died in March. After serving as vice president (October 2012-March 2013), Maduro became the interim president following Chávez's death. A zealous proponent of chavismo (the political system and ideology established by Chávez), Maduro was the successful candidate of the United Socialist Party of Venezuela (**Partido Socialista Unido** de Venezuela; PSUV) in the special election to replace Chávez, and he was reelected in 2018. Maduro's increasingly authoritarian rule led to repeated attempts by the opposition to remove him from office.

When Chávez died on March 5, 2013, it was the husky, mustachioed Maduro who made the announcement to the country. Earlier he had accused Venezuela's "imperialist" enemies of having poisoned Chávez. While interim president, Maduro ran against Capriles in the special election on April 14, 2013, to choose a president to serve out the remainder of Chávez's term. Maduro won the razor-close contest, capturing nearly 51 percent of the vote over just more than 49 percent for Capriles who was quick to make allegations of voting irregularities and to demand a full recount. Instead, the National Election Council chose to conduct an audit of the ballots in the 46 percent of precincts that had not already been automatically audited under Venezuela election law, though Capriles refused to participate in the audit and announced that he would undertake a legal challenge to the election results. Nevertheless, Maduro was sworn in as president on April 19th, 2013.

Despite U.S. sanctions, the country's worst economic crisis in history and dismal job approval ratings, Maduro, who has been president since 2013, has actually tightened his grip on power.

That dominance extended to last month's elections when pro-Maduro candidates swept races for governor and mayor. Noting that his Socialist Party has run the country for the past two decades, Maduro boasted in a Nov. 21 victory speech: *We are a major force in Venezuelan history.*

The Military Supports Maduro

His most important backing comes from the Venezuelan military, which in recent years has put down anti-government protests and stymied coup-plotters within its own ranks. Maduro has rewarded this loyalty by naming current of former military officers to head some ministries and to handle government food distribution.

These tasks provide openings for corrupt officers to fill their pockets, says Benjamin Scharifker, the former dean of Metropolitan University in Caracas. Another reason for sticking with Maduro, he says is that military commanders fear that under a new government they could go to prison for human rights violations, drug trafficking and other abuses.

The plunging economy hasn't toppled Maduro

Government mismanagement coupled with U.S. sanctions helped wreck Venezuela's economy. Since the end of 2013, the country's real gross domestic product has shrunk by almost 80%, estimates the International Monetary Fund.

But instead of weakening Maduro, the crisis has given his government more leverage over the population through its control of vital welfare programs, like monthly food handouts, says Temir Porras, a former top aide to Maduro.

"I think there is a misunderstanding that economic hardship [automatically] translates into political change," says Porras, who is now a visiting professor of political science at Sciences Po university in Paris. Instead, he says, *"the poorest of the Venezuelans become more dependent on any assistance they can get from government agencies."*

Meanwhile, oil production is starting to bounce back while the Maduro government also earns millions of dollars from gold mining.

"So, even though there are sanctions, even though there is a collapse of the economy, [Maduro] still has enough money to pay benefits to the military and to have support from the real powers," Scharifker says.

Caracas is now full of warehouses selling imported goods, which have alleviated some of the nation's food shortages. Also taking pressure off Maduro is the fact that nearly 6 million Venezuelans—about one-fifth of the pre-crisis population and many of whom oppose the president—have fled the country.

Over the past 5 years, Venezuelans have seen their quality of life deteriorate to previously unthinkable levels. In this once wealthy nation, today, almost 90% of the population lives in poverty. The root cause is inflation. *"Our money has turned into monopoly money."*

Hyperinflation has made the cost of food skyrocket. Hunger is widespread, and deaths from malnutrition are on the rise. One of the most popular items in the shops now is chicken skin, "we used to give them away for pets," said one butcher, shaking his head. "Now people seek them out."

As a result: millions of Venezuelan families are fleeing their country to escape starvation, violence, and disease.

- Venezuela's inflation rate has skyrocketed 53,000,000% since 2016
- 9 out of 10 people are trapped in starvation
- 64% of people have lost 25 lbs., on average, due to malnutrition
- 70% of Venezuela's hospitals have no water or electricity
- 5.3 million people fled Venezuela by the end of 2019 in 2017

Venezuelans began crossing the border looking for food and supplies as life in Venezuela was getting harder and harder. Businesses totally collapsed. Unemployment exceeded 80%. At this time, most people would cross the border by car or bus, buy food and supplies and then return home, as they did not expect to have to leave their country.

Most recently, people have had to walk as they cannot afford buses. Once they reach the Colombian border, refugees walk across mountainous terrain 700 km to Bogota, the capital and gateway to the rest of South America, or 500 km to Barranquilla, on the northern coast.

Chávez and Maduro gave the Venezuelan people "subsidies" or "free stuff" like free gas, free money, free food, free goods and services which caused inflation to rise so much their money became no good. So be wary if anyone offers you "free" things. Nothing in life is free, someone ultimately is paying for it, if not you are in the end!

THE UNITED STATES OF AMERICA

The term "capitalism" was almost unknown in the English world until first popularized by English translations of Marx's publication, *Das Kapital,* in 1867. The title was translated into English variously as *The Capital* or simply *Capital.* **Mercantilism** dominated the economic landscape in Europe during the sixteenth and seventeenth centuries and was the precursor to Capitalism.

In Marx's published work *Capital,* Volume 1 in 1867, it contains Marx's most fully developed thinking about the economics of modern capitalism: *"That capital is that of the commodity, as a useful object that may be exchanged on the market that stems from a need, from the stomach, or the imagination, makes no difference. This object becomes a commodity and that it is a product of labor."* (Marx)

The USA is a Capitalist nation. What we know as "Capitalism" emerged from Marx's published work. It may tinge the ears at times meaning to be meant as a bad thing, as Karl Marx was the first person who actually described the word "Capitalist" and remember his idea of a "utopian" state is Communism. A better word for what we have in the USA meaning the same thing is:

A **FREE MARKET** Economy - **Free Enterprise System** - An economic system in which private business operates in competition and largely free of state control.

Wealth creates wealth. It is not helpful to be jealous, spiteful, and degrading towards wealthy people who have worked hard, created businesses, innovated new concepts, ideas, and products to create their wealth. Nor is it helpful to take other people's wealth away. Many times, the businesses entrepreneurs start create many jobs for many people, thus, as stated above, "wealth creates wealth".

It is a place where competition can flourish: *"When most people discuss the "free market," they mean an economy with unobstructed competition"* thereby creating better products and a healthier economy (that is why you see at least 10 brands of macaroni and cheese in the grocery store and over 100 cereal selections). My niece, Reagan says: "In order for communism to truly thrive, you would have to be a minimalist. You can't be Madonna; you can't be a Material Girl." (RKT)

Two reasons why it is not a good idea to take wealth away from the wealthy: How much wealth you take away from wealthy people, (or the 1%, as has been coined in recent years) it is never or not enough to sustain the social programs and expensive give away government programs that socialists hope to achieve. 1% of people in America cannot take care of 331 million people (Worldometer population estimation in 2020) in the United States. No matter how many millions or billions they have, even if you take away ALL their money it will not be enough. Middle classes will be affected.

It will take away incentive: if everyone gets paid the same thing, or has the same wage, why work hard to achieve? No one will want to get higher educations and invest their money into start-up companies if their opportunities and monies earned will be overtaxed as soon as they become successful, and if a doctor is paid the same wage as a janitor. And if everyone is economically "equal" why would people have incentive to work hard and achieve success if it is taken away? People will not want to work hard to achieve, why not stay home? Do as your neighbor does? In a socialist society there is no benefit to hard work and innovation.

Also, since 2001, the share of federal income taxes paid by the top 1 percent increase from 33.2 percent to a new high of **40.1** percent in 2018.

In 2018, the top 50 percent of all taxpayers paid **97.1** percent of all individual income taxes, while the bottom 50 percent paid the remaining 2.9. percent.

This means the top earning Americans are *ALREADY* paying the most in taxes. They are the ones supporting those families in need of public assistance.

Countries that rejected socialism: The UK, India and Israel

The Entrepreneurial Spirit

ENTREPRENEUR: (OF ENTERPRISE)

en·tre·pre·neur
/ˌäntrəprəˈnər, ˌäntrəprəˈno͞o(ə)r/

Noun:

A person who organizes and operates a business or businesses, taking on greater than normal financial risks in order to do so. *"Many entrepreneurs see potential in this market"*

Similar:

a promoter in the entertainment industry. "The music entrepreneur pulled back from financing a screenplay Hopper had written"

An **entrepreneur** can make or sell commodities (products) like:

- Bread
- Cookies
- Spaghetti Sauce
- Homemade Pasta
- Fried Chicken (Like Colonel Sanders)
- Music Albums (Like your Aunt Kitty)
- Books
- Plays
- Medical tools

- Sports equipment or attire
- Energy tools like oil bits and tools (Like your Pau Pau)
- Video Games
- Cheesecakes
- Pillows
- Rocks/Crystals
- Bicycles
- Guitars
- Clothing/Hand Bags/Accessories/Jewelry
- Ice Cream

And many more things! Anything you can think of! AND Sell!

Not everybody is or can be an entrepreneur, but you can find your niche, or passion and create!

Other options are:

A Postal Worker- if you choose you can work for the government in a helpful way
A Banker
A Geographer (like your dad)
A Public Servant or work in the Political Realm or in Public Relations (like Papa)
An Actor
A Teacher
A Business Owner (Can also be under Entrepreneur)
A Businessperson working for a small or large private company (Like Laura, & Aunt Kitty)
An Accountant
A Computer Programmer/Technician/Coder/Website Designer
A Singer
A Cook/Chef
Fireman/Police Officer
A Writer
A Real Estate Agent

A Hostess

A Party Planner

A Diplomat

A Restauranteur

An Inventor

A Landowner

A Farmer

A Soldier: Like Uncle Abby: Senior Chief Albert Schneider USN Navy Seal,
Uncle: Major Geoff Templeton US Army, Cousin: Staff Sergeant George
Becton Templeton II US Army, Lieutenant Lewis Luth US Army, Major
Michael Luth US Army, Patrick A. Templeton First Lieutenant Army
Air Traffic Coordinating Officer Travis Air Force Base California

A Pilot

A Film and/or Theater Production Crew/

An Engineer

Movie Director (Like your Great Grandfather Pa Dink Templeton)

Stage Manager

AND more!

The good thing is in America you can do most anything you want. If you study and work hard you can achieve your goals and find a way to live. If you follow your passion, you can open up your own doors! In the USA there are opportunities for **upward mobility,** meaning you can start with nothing and work your way up. Some start more fortunate than others, but everybody has an **equal** opportunity to achieve a much happier and successful life: DO SOMETHING! *The more you do, the more you can do. It's a snowball effect.* (SDB) Whatever it is it is your choice. That is the beauty of America we are free to make our own decisions.

Some people take many years to find that thing that you are good at and love to do but try things. Find a way to live, and love, and be helpful and kind to others, with work, tenacity, purpose, and patience you can achieve! The key to success, according to Robert Moehling of the tropical Fruit Market, "Robert Is Here" is: *"Honesty, Integrity, and Hard Work. You can be honest every day, you can say what you're going to do, and have the Integrity to do it, and you can work hard the very first day you work."*

And maybe you WILL achieve wealth and stability and make a better life for yourself! And a better life, may not be weighed in dollars and cents, it may be achieved with love, compassion, partnership, teamwork, and a "Rich Life" can be achieved by being a good person, and being happy with what you have and what you can be, you do not need to be a millionaire to have a rich life, and be happy.

AUNT KITTY'S PHILOSOPHY:

The key is to have a meaningful and happy life, which is an opportunity we have in the USA. The more you do, the happier you can be! "Busy-ness" - have a job, be in school, learn something, read, write, find out things, be a part of clubs, whether it be drama clubs, soccer clubs, softball clubs, computer clubs, book clubs, bands, writing or poetry clubs, garden clubs, cooking for loved ones, find out what happens when you use the air fryer to dehydrate your homemade noodles, follow your passion, find friends, family, be involved, network, meet people, participate. Have fun! *"The business of America is business."* -Calvin Coolidge

"Innovation is still Capitalism's Star". "I think that America's business success through the decades has occurred because we have so many people with specialized knowledge who are willing to put their money, time and resources on the line for an idea that can't be proved to a committee" (Shiller).

Examples: Rhythm and Blues, Buddy Holly and Rock and Roll, the assembly line (Ford cars), M&M candy's, advances in Medicine (advancement in HIV/Aids curing by 2030), the I-phone, the Internet, Efficient Farming and Agriculture, Alternative Energy, Medical Vaccines, SpaceX, the future in Carbon Capture and much more! America is a pioneer in innovation.

By assuming the autonomy of the individual, capitalism grants dignity to the poor. By affirming people's rights to their own labor, regardless of their position on the economic ladder, capitalism offers the poor the means to improve their well-being. As many in history have experienced, capitalism is the ideal economic system for the people around the world. Again, capitalism produces wealth and innovation, improves the lives of individuals, and gives power to the people.

Two Stories

Let me tell you the stories of the upbringing and childhood of two of America's presidents: President Dwight D. Eisenhower and Barack Obama:

President Dwight D. Eisenhower: He wasn't an exceptional student or particularly promising military candidate. Yet he went on to become Supreme Allied Commander, assemble the greatest fighting force in the history of mankind, defeat Adolf Hitlers' war machine, save Western Civilization from fascism, and manage to get elected president twice by decisive majorities. He was from a small town, Abilene, Kansas, the heartland where his father worked as a mechanical engineer, putting in twelve- hour days, six days a week. He was the third of seven brothers in his family. He relished the rural life and would often go on hunting and fishing trips with friends. The Eisenhower household was a striving mixture of religious fundamentalism and the all-American ethos of Individualism and work ethic.

President Barak Obama: His Mom a white American from Kansas, married Barack Obama, Sr a black Kenyan who divorced his mom and moved back to Kenya and died 19 years later in a car accident. His Mom remarried an Indonesian foreign student. He was sent to school in Hawaii. "I was raised as an Indonesian child and a Hawaiian child and as a black child and as a white child. *And what I benefited from is a multiplicity of cultures that all fed me.*" (Barack Obama) He was a good but not outstanding student at Punahou. He played Varsity basketball. His Mom taught him: "to be black was to be the beneficiary of a great inheritance, a special destiny, glorious burdens that only we were strong enough to bear." Obama would then become the first black American president who was elected twice by decisive victories.

Both of these men grew up not terribly privileged and with difficulties, but it goes to show that it doesn't matter where you come from in America, but what you *can* be. You can be from a poorer community, you can come from a split home, you can come from different backgrounds, and we can never know who the next President will be and what his or her background did to shape them to be a great leader. Every person is different, and with different chances, utilize what you have, and good things will come! That is the Great American Story.

The Comparison between Free Market and Socialism

The thing about a Socialist Society is taxes go up on the American taxpayer to fund social programs for everybody. And if ultimate socialism, or in communist society you will most likely be working for the state, or there will be no incentive to work because the benefits go collectively to the community. There are no private businesses, all business is owned by the government in a socialist state. And the government oversees you from "womb to tomb", meaning starting to take care of you from birth, with government childcare, to public schooling; education, to a job working for an industry of government to then retire on government aid- to the tomb, the state putting you in the ground. In this instance, the state will tell you what kind of health care you will have, what your wages will be, and what to think as children, you will be indoctrinated to the state. In a socialist state there will be lines and a lot of wait time, as government programs can be very slow. *"Once government gets ahold of health care it's nothing but bureaucracy and red tape."* (BD) In the Soviet Union people had to stand in "bread lines".

Representative Alexandria Ocasio-Cortez's proposal of the "GREEN NEW DEAL" on February 7th, 2019, is a red herring for a new government system; or reorganizing the free market and entrepreneurial system into a state-run socialist society, in response to "climate change." President Biden has adopted this agenda, and it is partly because of the GREEN NEW DEAL elements in the Infrastructure Investment and Jobs Act 11/15/21-Public Law No: 117-58 that your gas and food prices are so high. Biden's administration has cut back the American Energy Sector (gas and oil) to implement their green agenda." *We need to turn back on the gas spicket. The Biden Administration has caused a large chunk of this inflation its primarily energy based, and so if we turn on the gas spicket again get those prices down all that translates into a loaf of bread. Because the loaf of bread has to be delivered with gasoline and paid for with 20$ an hour people that used to make 10 dollars an hour people, so this is what's causing inflation."* (Dave Ramsey) Biden's Administration want to force you to pay higher prices so they can control you. White House advisor Brian Deese claims high gas prices are necessary for the 'future of the liberal world order'.

"You can't control the environment. You'll find things like fossils on the top of the Grand Canyon and realize Arizona used to be under an ocean… and then realize climate change is pretty normal for the earth." (Pavlich) A world where we would be "slaves" to the state and government where the laws that government provides would make the world better according to them and not you, the people.

"What is it about that [Marx] philosophy that has been so enduring? When it constantly promises Heaven, but delivers Hell?" (Hegseth) Don't ever let your elected representatives tell you what is best for YOU and how to live properly. It is up to YOU in a free country, in America, how you want to live your life, or what to believe, not the government. "And if you live in a poor inner city where there are no goods and high crime you don't care what the weather will be in 50 years, 'climate change' is the greatest white privilege in the world". (Failla)

You have the right to protect your freedom with your 2nd Amendment right to bear arms. That is exactly to protect yourself from the government gone awry, like it did in Venezuela, the most recent example when Maduro got elected in to power by 1.49% of the vote, or fewer than 225,000 votes.

Socialism was voted in in Venezuela, and accompanied by cheers and hoorahs, and claps and crowds of happy people voting in the socialist candidate only to watch their beloved, rich country turn into a wasteland of nothingness in a matter of less than 5 years, with no food, or medicine, and under the control of a military power and Maduro's dictatorship.

Venezuela was the wealthiest Latin American country at the turn of the Millennium until Maduro came into power in 2013 (see the animated movie "Up" as recent as 2009, when Venezuela was still an attractive destination) now people are fleeing the country by any means possible.

Socialism can be voted in with cheers and great applause but will have to be fought out of with guns, firepower, and resolve, after being left with nothing, but in Venezuela citizens do not have guns. Don't let the politicians take away your guns! No matter what.

"Freedom is a fragile thing and it's never more than one generation away from extinction. It is not ours by way of inheritance; it must be fought for and defended constantly by each generation, for it comes only once to a people. And those in world history who have known freedom and then lost it have never known it again." - Ronald Reagan

In these times we are living, USA is dangerously close to becoming a socialist country. The Left is going hard winged radical to socialist with Left-wing Democrat politicians like Senator Bernie Sanders, and "the Squad:" Alexandria Ocasio-Cortez (AOC), Ilhan Omar, Rashida Tlaib, Ayanna Pressley, Jamaal Bowman, and Cori Bush, who are Progressive, Far Left, Democrats in the House of Representatives.

President Biden, who is a puppet pulled by the Progressive wing to bend to Leftist Party Politics and promoters, was sold to America by propaganda in the Mainstream Media as being a "moderate", which he is not.

When President Biden asked the question in his January 19th, 2022, Press Conference: *"What do Republicans stand for?"* Republican Senator John Barrasso replied: *"We stand for jobs, we stand for a strong economy, we stand for national security, which is energy security, border security, military security."*

Biden went so far to the Left, a freight train to the Left with Pelosi, Biden, and Schumer proposing things that are really radical, extreme, dangerous, scary; massive spending, massive taxes, and massive regulations things that are going to make it much harder for our economy to recover..." (Senator John Barrasso R-WY)

"The Mainstream Media is the marketing branch of the Democratic Party" (Watters), and yes, even on our campuses and schools, and your schools, will teach you that Socialism and Communism is a great idea, and they will not teach the History or current events of the 4 Examples I have laid out in the premise that Russia, China, Nazi Germany, and Venezuela

by Stalin, Mao Zedong and the CCP, Hitler, and Maduro all came to power under the guise of **socialism**, and strength through community economic equality. Your teachers will try to persuade you and encourage you to believe false promises of a utopian classless society. Why should the rich be rich? As I have explained why they should be earlier in this paper. If the rich are not rich, nobody will be rich. There will be no money for anyone.

"Capitalism is not these big corporations. Capitalism is the small business owners, it's the person that started it out of the basement of their home or garage and now own a small business that employs 4 people, that's not possible in any other system but the capitalist-free enterprise system". (Senator Marko Rubio R-Fl)

I do not care how much Bernie can 'discuss' and wave his hands on his utopia-fairy tale 'Robin Hood' communist philosophy, and what color AOC's lipstick and matching outfit is, and her "Tax the Rich" evening gown. The rich are already being taxed! Bernie Sanders and The Squad are socialists, wolves in sheep's clothing, and they are disguising themselves in the Democrat party! They are out to utterly change the USA into something that is unrecognizable! Next thing you know they will bear a different flag. Bernie Sanders, and Alexandria Ocasio-Cortez are Socialists, looking to grow government and their power, they are socialists, if not total **communists**, even though the American system has gotten them to where they are today. Ironically, communism is the very thing the USA has been fighting over 70 years that is now prominently campaigned for in the Democratic Party in the USA! Have we forgotten? Yes.

Why?

One reason could be that many, though not all, of the younger generation, are content to be taken care of, after they have finished secondary school by 18. They then want the state (or their parents) to continue to take care of them into their adult life, take care of their debts, put them through college, graduate school, Law school, Master Programs take care of their health, take care of their children. They are not ready to grow up, take care of their own lives, garner lives and responsibilities of their own, instead live in the womb of the state.

More reasons why Bernie Sanders is so appealing are: Bernie Sanders is an "Authentic Social Justice Warrior" and because "Radicalism is Romantic" (Gutfeld). Many people of all ages, think this false promise: that taking from the rich will somehow equal more money for their pockets.

People think it's great to be a socialist, it is my theory: that people do not **understand** what Socialism really is. I have seen young people asking this question. And in this paper, I am trying in the simplest way to answer this question.

Another reason socialism is appealing may be because there is great wealth disparity in the United States. There are homeless people, at the same time as there are multi billionaires. Some people might think: how can this be? It isn't fair. It is a thought of many of the poorest: that it's the rich people's fault they are poor. They don't know that it's those very people that offer jobs, employment, security, education, and **upward mobility** to the poorest communities. Historically, millionaires/billionaires like Walt Disney, Henry Ford, Chrysler, Howard Hughes, Bill Gates (founder of Microsoft), Ted Turner (founder of Cable News Network; CNN) Jeff Bezos (founder of Amazon and owner of The Washington Post), Steve Jobs, and Elon Musk have created large American companies where people can work and advance themselves. This is where dreams are built and made, and futures are designed. *"This is who we are as a country and every American benefits."* (Bruce)

Representative Alexandria Ocasio Cortez is the District Representative of one of the poorest districts of New York, and in America, the 14th District. New York's 14th District represents more than 650,000 people across parts of the Bronx and Queens. It was early 2019 when Amazon decided not to build a corporate campus in Queens, NYC. *"After community backlash, Amazon has decided not to move forward with its plan to open a headquarters in Long Island City, Queens."* Instead of the idea of gaining advancement through employment, what Alexandria Ocasio Cortez had to offer, a socialist platform of a promise of free government programs, and subsidies became more appealing. The Amazon Company was going to offer jobs in a community that would have benefitted from more jobs. Somewhere around 80% of Bronx residents receive some form of public assistance. Alexandia Ocasio Cortez stopped Amazon from coming into her District, New York's 14ᵗʰ District, and it still remains one of the poorest Districts in America.

Many who call themselves "Progressives" do in fact believe social programs are the answer. These youths weren't around during the Cold War against the Soviet Union (1946-1991), they have not traveled to Venezuela. And let's have all things free; education, health insurance, free women's contraception, but the toss up is: do you really want the government to be making all the decisions for you for the rest of your life? Do you want exorbitantly high taxes? Do you want to be in the same economic category as everybody else? Do you want to drive the same car as your neighbor? If you are even able to have a car at all? Do you want rows and rows of the same product on the shelves of your grocery store (Like in Cuba)? Do you want the government regulating things you say? And giving you only news that you are allowed to hear like in Russia, "*Pravda*"- newspaper meaning "*Truth*"?

This is now the mainstream belief in the Democratic Party. "*They woke up one day I guess and decided that Marxism was right all along and that the Cold War should have never ended, and I don't understand how people that feel that way don't move to other countries, there are so many countries out there that agree with that sentiment about socialism being better than capitalism.*" (Senator Marko Rubio R-Fl) Then vote for a Socialist. You will lose your Liberty. You will be told what to do and censored like in Communist China. "*They do not want children to have a mind of their own.*" (Schneider) No more free thought. Everybody will be the same, with no chance for upward mobility or chance to gain success, unless you are in the secret police, or (SS) like in Nazi Germany, or a "henchman" that Stalin used, or a government insider of a person who is in control like in Venezuela where the militia is well paid to keep Maduro in power, or a member of the communist party (CCP). But chances are you will not be in that class. You will be a regular person, like everybody else in oppression, like most people in these types of states live, or leave, if they can. But where would you go?

"*Because socialism is not about economics, It's about power. The ability to control people, if you can control where people work, how much they make,*" *who owns what, then you can control what they can say, who they can hire, what they can sell, what hours they can open its about power and control, and it's about a government in control of every aspect of your life."* (Senator Marko Rubio R-Fl)

Be careful, as going through schools and higher education, the Left is teaching students socialist ideologies in elementary, secondary school, colleges, and masters programs, all the way up to doctorate programs teaching that the USA is determinably bad, and evil, with our riches and wealth, and our history.

In fact, the more "higher education" you get the more *liberal* you become in most cases. It creeps into you without you even knowing. We are not bad. We are good! And the USA, and many other Capitalist, and Free Market countries, will have to continue on to be good and vigilant with people electing leaders who believe in a FREE MARKET Economy, and yes Capitalism! And yes, Capitalism is not perfect, as nothing is perfect, but it is far better than the alternative, it provides advancement and opportunity to citizens. America is the final frontier of freedom. Once America is gone, it will be GONE. So, protect her as much as you possibly can!

And I warn you, we are not as free as we once used to be, the **conservative** population has all but been silenced. One of our 1st Amendment Rights: the right to Freedom of Speech, is being trampled on by violent groups like ANTIFA: "Anti-Fascists" violent masked Leftists, who beat up and push conservative voices out of college campuses using mindless and casual labeling: racist/sexist/hater/xenophobic to stop them from speaking, and hecklers at open town halls to disrupt, ugliness and bullying on Twitter. *"Facebook and Twitter they are the 19th Century Robber Barrons."* (Victor Davis Hanson)

They are condemning Elon Musk for wanting to buy Twitter so he can bring back free speech to the platform. Max Boot says: "For democracy to survive, we need more content moderation, not less." (Boot) *"Content moderation" it sounds really good, but it's a euphemism for censorship."* (Gutfeld) "I have a theory, at first, I thought that these people were all over reacting having this massive freakout over this small problem, but then I started thinking maybe they are freaking out because it is bigger than we know… their reaction is an acknowledgement that they are doing more things like gatekeeping then we realize. Because a lot of times when someone has an irrational reaction, you just don't know the whole story." (Timpf) *"Democrats want to control what is said and what is not said. That's why corporate America, social media, is trying so hard to maintain their grip on power to the point where entities like Twitter is doing what is averse to their shareholder's interest to keep Elon Musk out."* (McEnaney)

Now, the Biden Administration has plans to set up a "Disinformation Board," in the department of Homeland Security, which if you have read George Orwell's book, "1984", you will find frightening similarities of this government Disinformation Board to Orwell's "Ministry of Truth" government branch. *"The Party told you to reject the evidence of your eyes and ears. It was their final, most essential command."* (George Orwell) There should NEVER be a board or department like this in the American government.

Cancel Culture is set to silence conservative publications, voices, businesses, and jobs, and censorship of conservative groups on Facebook, YouTube, and Twitter of people discussing all topics freely like Joe Rogan, asking questions about Covid. Ironic, isn't it? They will tell you only what they want you to know about Covid. Questioning their information is not allowed. There cannot be any questions.

"All of a sudden now Liberals are saying they are afraid that people with different political views on the Left might get canceled on Twitter, voices might be silenced. Well, where have you been these last numbers of years because conservatives have been living this nightmare for the entire time. And not one of these people one time ever stood up and said: *"what you are doing by banning Donald Trump, whether you like him or not, is wrong."* (Hannity)

The very faction that claims to be anti-fascism, is the very fascist party itself in shutting down free speech and supporting violence on voices of political opponents! In what era did we think that a President of the United States would be banned from speaking on an American platform? He was banned because he was a political opponent. If a President, can be banned from Twitter so, can you, so can YOU, your ideas, your thoughts, and your communications.

"The real danger that we're facing as a society right now in this country is that this fundamental freedom guaranteed to every one of us as Americans, freedom of speech, is being threatened, people are being intimidated, their financial security is being threatened. They are being censored or being intimidated to censor themselves. This freedom is the fabric of our Constitution, and the fact that this is what we're facing, that the powers that be decided if we don't like the things you are saying, then we will silence you and censor you..."

"We need to have the confidence in America that we can express ourselves, that we have the freedom to speak without the threat of punishment looming over us. That right there is literally the difference of living in a Democracy or a Dictatorship" (Tulsi Gabbard) Freedom of Speech is a First Amendment right.

The people see what is going on, and this faction in the US, who is Leftist, and Radical Left, is trying to already silence your voice, just like Stalin silenced so many in the Great Purge in his own government in the USSR by murdering those in political opposition, and dissent. He did not let anyone have a differing political voice. Again, a reason to keep your arms. Be able to fight back if need be! Do not let, under any circumstances anyone take away your guns, or your rights, or your VOICE! *"We're all free spirits! I can agree with you on one issue, and you on another and guess what... I'm a free agent with my own thought process!"* (Curtis Sliwa) *"And somehow those are endangered."* (Gutfeld)

"We have some really difficult challenges. If you look at the threats to freedom it's not just within the Federal Government and the Biden Administration, but you have a Corporate America now that is embracing "wokeness", the ideology that that entails, the Universities have gotten way more Left wing, just even in that last 20 years. Then you look at Big Tech, which is basically taking the authority to suffocate dissent and try to foster a narrative, and I don't even have to discuss the corporate media and how dishonest they have been.

If you believe in the core principles that has made the country great and if you believe in those core values you are under assault from a wide range of Institutions now, that may be different now then the threats we faced when Reagan was President or some of the other past cycles because the rot in some of the culture I don't think was as severe as now." (Governor Ron Desantis)

"What is going on with society...? "Woke" everything-if you don't agree with me, if you say what you say, you don't have a right to say it anymore." (Ari Fleischer)

Tucker Carlson explained censorship in this way: *"Weak people are for censorship - I can't handle what you are throwing at me- shut up or else... strong people don't behave that way."*

You might think that it is dramatic to compare the Left to Joseph Stalin, and the censorship of conservative voices of today, but it's a slippery hill... once certain rights are removed, further actions can sometimes follow... Silencing political opponents is already very un-American, and it is now in practice currently in the USA. There are still over 600 January 6th, 2021, protesters over a year after the incident, being jailed in solitary confinement, under horrible 3rd world conditions in jails in DC and VA, who are suffering from: denial of medical care, physical abuse, sleep disruption, verbal intimidation threats, denial of religious practices, and malnutrition. Only one-tenth of the trials have commenced (71 out of 725) while the other nine-tenths people are just being left there to rot in these jails, some of these political prisoners are being sentenced to up to 5 years in prison all for committing the "crime" of political dissent.

Is that the free country you would like to be living in where people are being jailed indefinitely for speaking their voice? Their right to assembly? This sounds an awfully lot like Russia and China. But it's happening here.

AUNT KITTY'S JOURNEY

My voice has come in the form of voting for Presidential elections, writing, and singing. In 1992, when I was a high school senior, I registered to vote in my English class. I registered as a Democrat. My first vote in 1992, when I was 18 years old, I voted for the "outsider" Ross Perot, a wealthy Individual who ran for President from a grassroots party called "The Reform Party" to shake up the Establishment. Perot believed Americans were disillusioned with the state of politics as being corrupt and unable to deal with vital issues. He did not win, nor did the Republican Incumbent George Bush, Sr. that was the year Bill Clinton came into power. I didn't vote anytime during Clinton's Presidency, nor did I vote in the 2000 election between George W. Bush and Al Gore. In 2004, I was adamantly opposed to a War with Iraq, so I then went back to the voting booth and voted against George W. Bush for his opposition, John Kerry, who did not end up winning. And George W. Bush ended up winning a second term and we invaded Iraq.

Then in 2008 I voted for Barack Obama for President, a lot of people did, he was charismatic, and I think a lot of Americans wanted a black president, with new ideas, and a message of change. I was impressed by him, he spoke well, and I liked his Progressive stance on gay marriage, giving the LGBT community more rights.

I voted for Obama again, for his second term in 2012. I was pleased with the gas prices being low, and more people had healthcare than before, from what I heard. But there was some sort of unsatisfaction during this time, the country had become more divisive, people began to hate America. *"The Obamas were the creators and starting point of all the division and current anti-American chaos we're witnessing in America today"*. (Lomax) President Obama continually went abroad and apologized for America.

That always made me scratch my head, *what was wrong with America*? I thought.

The Black Lives Matter movement made police the "bad" guys, racial tensions went through the roof, the word 'white' became a bad word, and the seeds were planted for the "defund the police" movement and the war on cops, in the economy things had not improved, as far as money in my wallet, food prices went up, jobs opportunities were scarce, and in general I had been unemployed 6 of the 8 years while Obama was in office. I finally got a job in 2015. I never did tip well during this time because I didn't have the money to tip well if I went out for dinner or drinks, which was sparingly at best.

Then one summer day, my brother picked me up on our way to our summer vacation in Virginia, summer 2016, and he had Rush Limbaugh on the car radio and everything Rush said made sense to me! I couldn't believe it! The rumblings of discontent that I felt all made sense while listening to this conservative talk show commentator! Finally, someone who still "liked" America!

Then Donald Trump came onto the scene and announced his bid for candidacy for President, he made it to the debate stage, and I was curious to see him. I had never watched him on his widely popular TV show "The Apprentice" and up to that point never really thought much about him, even though he was already a Public Figure in our culture. I thought he was kind of tacky with all the gold about and trimmings, not really my taste. But what he said on that debate stage I understood! I could tell he loved America too with his 'America First' agenda. His slogan for the 2016 campaign was "Make America Great Again!" And it really resonated with me, and I watched further, through the Republican Convention, and I see now, the years I emersed myself in Russian History, it all became clear. The current events happening in Venezuela figured prominently, and Trump's idea of "law and order" and secure borders resonated with me. And I have always loved America, I consider myself to be a patriotic American.

While I was on welfare with my disability, trying to keep my head above water, illegal immigrants were pouring into this country (by the millions), taking our jobs, getting on subsidies, our services, and doing their thing, with no regard for our language and our system of law, at the same time I couldn't even get certain services that I needed. I thought;

"there's got to be some law and order here!" And President Trump was able to deliver a plan of the wall, I was and am strongly in support of that.

While politics had become a stalemate of 'just another day in DC' Trump came in as an outsider, to shake up the DC establishment. All the way back to Ross Perot, I had commented earlier, I have always been in support of the "outsider." Now, I was in support of Donald Trump. I do not trust career politicians; they give you a lot a sweet talk, but nothing gets done.

The Hillary Clinton campaign was ridden with corruption, the Hawks of the George W. Bush Presidency were still establishment types. And Obama, left the country so divided. When Trump came in one of his goals was to rid DC from the corruption of many years of political gain of prominent political figures, DC bureaucratic pundits, and the elites to *"Drain the Swamp!"* (Donald Trump)

The establishment hate him so much, as do the mainstream media because he is their biggest threat! And I'm sick of it as are a lot of Americans, and Trump supporters and the average American, believe that it's time to not be the forgotten men and women, and let our voices be heard, and our needs be met! I voted Republican in 2016.

Now our country is safe. The threat of terror, from Isis, and Iran are deluded, from the disaster that was the Iraq War, when those problems arose. And now people are working, making money, I find I am tipping better, and more often, because I have money in my pocket. I cannot afford to travel abroad on my own right now, but my income is ok. I am off of food stamps, and I am paying for my own Dental and Vision insurance at a competitive low cost. The good thing about having a job, is that you can pay for your own food! These are things I am realizing getting off the state.

I took an eight-day trip to California on my own. I took a plane to visit childhood friends in South Carolina for my birthday. I am more independent! I couldn't be happier, realizing many of my fellow Americans are doing and feeling the same things. We've got to keep this economic boom, and strength up! What a wonderful country we live in when our biggest decision of the night is whether we will have flat or drumstick chicken wings for the Superbowl!

Fast Forward to 2022

Now I am unemployed. On the 15th of March 2020 I lost my job due to the Corona Virus Pandemic, (the very next day after I had finished the first final draft of this paper, see above). Just about two years later I find myself very much stuck on the government. I have been receiving food stamps and am back on full government health insurance with Medicare and Medicaid. I received PUA (Pandemic Unemployment Assistance) from Sept 2020 until March of 2021, and am living off that savings, and my disability SSI income. My current work is the project to finish this book. I have found I can write, and it is now my dream to inform the youth of America, and anyone who wants to learn, about socialism and to turn my own books/music/poetry into capital for my own business. I have already been investing in my own products (my 3 music CD's) for almost 20 years. One day I am hoping for a bit of a return. It is time for me to take a chance on America, and this Free Enterprise System and go for it! There are obstacles to overcome, in any endeavor, but I am banking on this country still being in one piece by the time this book comes out and taking a chance on myself!

The money I have to invest in this book project came directly from my PUA Pandemic Unemployment Assistance after I lost my job at the Great Escape Room in March of 2020 due to the Corona Virus Pandemic. I was able to save up a chunk of my PUA due to being locked down, more money was coming in than going out at that time, and thanks to President Trump I am able to have the capital I need to publish this book. It was under his Presidency people who needed assistance, and earned it, got it. My PUA ended in March of 2021, a little less than 2 months after Biden came into office. Since then, I have not seen any real financial help from the Biden Administration except for the regular minimal welfare due to my disability I have been receiving since 2007.

All these trillions of dollars floating around, and none of it is seeming to land on me. I have been trying for 15 years to get subsidized housing due to my disability, and never got even close. No one else in my case manager's MBI community, that she knows, has received a housing subsidy since Biden has been in office either. I am not sure where all the money goes? It is a mystery, I haven't seen it, nobody I know has seen it.

I come from an upper middle-class background, and I have been fortunate that my family was able to provide for me an education and has been supportive of me throughout my life. On my own, I have been living below the poverty line since my first years out of college, (income under 20,000$) and where I live now is one of the more affordable areas in DC.

I love it, but I have also seen some real things. I was able to produce my albums with money I made at several part time jobs I have had throughout the years. My most recent job I had for almost 5 years, until the Pandemic closed our doors, was at the DC location of The Great Escape Room in Dupont Circle. At that time, I experienced things like being able to buy better and more expensive gifts for my family at Christmas, and simple travel. And during the past 5 years of gainful employment, I have been happy. I am not a rich person, but I have a "Rich Life" a simple life enjoying small pleasures like friends, family, cooking, music and poetry.

I did not go to graduate school because I did not want to accrue debt, and there was no field I wanted to go in specifically to further in my education. So, I did not go. Not to say, if later I find a new passion, I will make a way to go back to school or take classes, but I want to see what my four-year degree can do first. It is not up to the American taxpayer to pay for your college tuition. You can choose to attend a Community College, or a State University, Vocational School, Trade School, join the US Military, or apply for Apprenticeship Programs for discounted and reasonable prices in your area. It should not be up to the American taxpayer to pay for your elite education (Masters/Law School/Private Liberal Arts Schools/Doctorate and Ph. D. Programs). *"Forgiveness of college loans is a handout to the rich."* (Sean Duffy)

Now in 2022, the landscape of the country and the feelings around are not of the joy, happiness, and confidence that I expressed in certain parts of this paper anymore. It is questionable if we are even the #1 economy in the world, now that China has just caught up on us strategically, militarily, and just about economically. I don't even know where this country stands globally economically anymore. I do not feel particularly safe due to the Afghanistan debacle and the seemingly endless war in Ukraine. And people are feeling higher anxiety due to a rise in costs, rise in violent crime in cities, high inflation, higher gas prices, higher food prices, and empty shelves in grocery stores. *"The American economy is experiencing the highest inflation rate in 40 years since 1982"* (Baier). Now people can barely pay for food, and gas!

Now, the opportunity is ripe for the current Administration, the Biden Administration, to push heavy spending and get more people hooked on the government with his Build Back Better agenda which includes social and climate change policy which is riddled with handouts for special interest groups who want a piece of the pie. It is their goal to get citizens (and even non-citizens) hooked up on all the government programs so they can exert their control, power over you, and buy votes. It is President Biden who stopped the construction of the border wall his very first day in office January 20, 2021, (when he also ended America's projects in the energy, gas and oil sector).

In 2021, 1.7 million people flooded our border illegally, and that number is estimated to go up to 2.1 million people by the end of the 2022 Fiscal year according to Princeton Policy Advisors. Biden's Administration is letting everybody in with his 'Open Borders Policy' in hopes that they will in turn vote Democrat, because they already know they don't have enough votes to win the midterms, and probably not the 2024 Presidential elections because Biden is doing so abysmally as president in his first term.

Biden's DOJ (Department of Justice) is suing Arizona over "proof of citizenship voter law" which means his administration is trying to legalize illegal immigrants to vote. That is how desperate they are becoming. Already in NY a law that would have allowed non-citizens to vote in local election was struck down. *"There is no statutory ability for the city of New York to issue inconsistent laws permitting non-citizens to vote and exceed the authority granted to it by the New York State Constitution."* (Justice Ralph J. Porzio) According to the UN: "the U.S. Southern Border is the deadliest in the world". Not to mention the drugs spilling over killing our teens.

The people 'in charge' of what to do about Covid flips flops all the time and call it "science", and now, in DC I have to mask up every time I step out of my apartment. I get yelled at from strangers passing complaining if I am not fully masked up (mask shaming). Once I was called "*killer*" while walking down my floor hallway in my pajamas late at night taking my trash out without my mask. Nice. It is a sure different environment than it was even just a couple of years ago. I cannot walk the halls of my building without a mask. Now I cannot go anywhere [in DC] without showing my 'vax papers.' People are getting murdered blocks away from where I am dining. Things are not normal. Shocking because this is not the America I grew up in.

Crime is at an all- time high. "The liberal leaders are governing cities where hard working Americans taxpayers do not want to live in a dangerous, violent, filthy, expensive hell hole whether it is San Francisco or New York." (McDowell) "76% of New Yorkers are in fear that they will be a victim of violent crime. *If you don't' have safety, you have nothing."* (Cain)

Biden has issued a government mandate that is being fought in the courts, that all companies that employ over 100 employees, and all Military and Federal workers, and all Medical workers MUST get the vaccine if not that is grounds for termination. This is clearly an unconstitutional mandate, that in a free country, mandates like this must not pass. June 30th, 2022, was the deadline to get the vaccine for the Military, and 40,000 US Service men and women chose not to get the vaccine, which is 13%. Now the government does not know what to do with them, this mandate is grounds for termination. Is Biden going to fire 40,000 brave Americans in our Military because they didn't want the shot? We don't know how many Medical/Care workers and Federal workers got the boot because of this mandate either.

People are losing their jobs, their livelihoods, their security! Citizens should make decisions for themselves and their health individually and with their doctors in a free society, not the government!

In schools, kids are having to be masked up all day, and be susceptible to ideological teachings like CRT (Critical Race Theory), which in it of itself is a "theory", that divides children on their skin color from who is the "oppressed" and who is the "oppressor." Children are too young to realize this notion! "Kids don't see color, why force them to?" (Frederick Douglas) It is teaching kids to hate each other! Nothing that has come before them is their fault! *"Critical race Theory is nothing more than state sanctioned racism."* (Pence) It is the very opposite of the teachings of Martin Luther King, Jr. who said:

"So even though we face the difficulties of today and tomorrow, I still have a dream. It is a dream deeply rooted in the American dream… I have a dream that my four little children will one day live in a nation where they will not be judged by the color of their skin but the content of their character. I have a dream today." - Martin Luther King, Jr

Schools were supposed to receive billions in aid with the passing of The American Rescue Plan Act so teachers could get back into the classroom to teach in person, yet teachers still walked out and held strikes in Chicago, and several other parts of the country where teachers tried to go back to virtual learning. What happened to that assurance? *"Within 30 days of receiving funds, develop and publish plans to safely reopen schools for in-person instruction."* (Public Law No: 117-2 (03/11/2021- American Rescue Plan Act)

It is clear Americans are living with higher anxiety than just in the past 2 years. And there are several reasons for this anxiety, as I have stated above, but in most instances where you talk to people, they are bewildered and unsure of the future. They are frustrated, disappointed, and nervous of Biden's Administration. Living is getting expensive, and there's no relief in sight. It is not the best of times we are living. But the good news is, which I cling onto, is that we have another opportunity to vote. It is 2022, and elections will be held in this upcoming November.

Also, in 2024 there will be a Presidential election, and we need to do our part as American citizens to vote in the people who we think will do the best job. And rest assured, I will not be voting for a Democrat. "They are the Democratic Socialist Party". (Jeff Van Drew) We need to get smart, strong people who care about this country back into leadership positions.

The Difference between Social Democracy in Europe, and Socialism Rearing its head in USA

Many people who are proponents of **Socialism** will tell you: "but look at Europe, the Nordic Countries their Social Democracy is working, so see how socialism is working?" It is not the same. The radical Left is controlling the Biden Administration to propose huge spending bills.

"President Joe Biden will propose $5 trillion in new federal spending over the next decade on Friday as part of his fiscal year 2022 budget request (Build Back Better)" which is really the "Green New Deal" cloaked in sheep's clothing, a massive social spending bill to mostly address climate change that America does not need and is not interested in. It is directed to give away a lot of social plans with a lot of "free stuff." No person in the world has that much money, no combined wealth of the wealthiest in the United States has that kind of money! Who do you think will pay for it? Just print more money? That will cause higher inflation. *"We are all paying back the free stimulus money now with inflation through the roof. This is the price we pay for free money. Nothing is free."* (Birch) "Instead, the smaller Infrastructure Investment and Jobs Act- 11/15/2021- Public Law No: 117-58 (for 1.85 Trillian dollars) passed.

"The obvious reason for inflation is because the government printed a zillion amount more money than it had. It's very basic, not super-complicated. Like in Venezuela, the poor people of Venezuela have been run roughshod by their government." (Elon Musk)

"When you put more money in the economy, you devalue the dollar and its worthless." (Sean Duffy) That's how we got so much inflation the first

place with all this spending, and there is no end in sight. Where did the money go? We know a half a trillion dollars of the American Rescue Act was stolen by foreign entities due to government money mis-management, and billions of dollars were supposed to go to schools for new ventilation systems. Where did that money go? Who did it go to? There is SO MUCH money floating around after the passing of the American Rescue Plan Act, and yet I am not sure where the money went. Do you know? *"This administration has made it very clear that the Green New Deal and Climate Change and billions of dollars running through DC is their agenda and they can care less about the American people, our food supply, our food security. I've always said: no farms, no food, no future"*. (Stephanie Nash)

Already the government has spent roughly 4 trillion dollars on Pandemic Relief (CARES ACT of 2020 (1.9 trillion) and (American Rescue Plan Act of 2021 (1.9 trillion)) and in passing the scaled down bipartisan infrastructure bill to 1.85 trillion adds up to nearly 6 trillion dollars of government spending in the past 2 years. And now to spend 5 trillion more? There is NO way we can afford all that, that kind of spending is out of control, it is causing mass inflation. *"From the time Biden's America Rescue Plan Act passed to today, inflation has consistently run ahead of wages and delivering a substantial pay cut to Americans, and everybody knows it."* (Perino) It goes far deeper than 'Putin's Price Hike'.

Thank God for Joe Manchin (D-WV), a Democrat who voted against the furthering of the 5 trillion part of Build Back Better bill and stopped it dead in its tracks. He did not vote with his party, he had a mind of his own, and knew what is better for his state of West Virginia, and the country. His vote was a "nay." He saved his party from themselves, and also potentially saved this country from a further disastrous economic free fall.

The countries in Europe would certainly not go for that kind of spending, or that kind of government control. "The UK's National Health Service does NOT ban private health insurance. Sweden has massive school choice and vouchers. Denmark has one of the lowest levels of government regulations in world." (Hilton). *"**Legos** and **IKEA** [In Denmark] are not brought to you by socialism, it is the **FREE MARKET** that makes that available to you"* (Anderson). These European countries are not fully socialist countries. They may have some socialist policies but are still Free Market economies.

Bernie Sanders is a Washington Insider, who spent very little time working in the private sector. Since he was elected Mayor of Burlington, Vermont in 1981 he has been a life-long politician. He has acquired 3 houses.

His summer house in Vermont is on an acre of waterside property and has 4 bedrooms, in all his worth is 2.5 million in assets from his career as a politician. He made the bulk of his money on book sales and deals. Sanders published three hit books in three years, from 2016 to 2018: *Our Revolution: A Future to Believe In, Bernie Sanders Guide to Political Revolution*, and finally *Where We Go from Here: Two Years in the Resistance.*

The first trip he took as a newlywed with his wife was to the Soviet Union at the height of the Cold War in 1988. He is a **Socialist** openly, and advocates for Marxism and a classless society here in the USA, yet he is living a rich man's life.

Biden, who campaigned on being a "moderate" democrat, is constantly being pulled to the Left by Bernie Sanders, AOC and the Squad, and even HIMSELF looking for government control and power, for his party. President Biden, Nancy Pelosi, and Chuck Schumer are wanting to pass legislation to Federalize elections. *"Today I am making it clear to protect our Democracy I support changing the Senate Rules, whichever way they need to be changed to prevent a minority of Senators to block voting rights!"* (President Joe Biden) In doing so they would have to change the Filibuster rule because they do not have enough votes to pass it, which is the: 'I am losing this game so I will change the rules now' philosophy; "fundamentally changing the Institution [of the Senate]." (Senator Mitch McConnell R-Ky)

Elections are determined by the States. This is a power grab of the Federal Government. The Biden Administration would like to fix the rules to give them the upper hand so their opposition, Republicans, never win elections again, and in that scenario, we would be a ONE-PARTY STATE. If you have picked up anything in this paper, it is that would scare you in and of itself. What is wrong with showing your ID at a voting station? You have to show your ID every time you get on an airplane or drive a car! It is not a big deal, and it is not a racial deal. Keep elections fair, and up to the individual State like it says in the Constitution.

The election should be held in one day like it has been traditionally held since our country was founded, and the results determined that same day to avoid *mules* stuffing the ballot drop boxes weeks in advance, like they did in 2020. The Covid Pandemic gave States an excuse to change voting rules suddenly and at the last minute, which paved the way to irregular voting procedures in the 2020 election. *"That was an election un-like any we have experienced in our history."* (Hemingway)

Now that the Covid Pandemic has subsided, we should go back to our long-standing way of holding an election in one day, where every American can go to the voting booth and vote, once. They are making "early voting" in drop boxes and "mail in ballots" (that are not Absentee Ballots) a regular thing. It is not. Wouldn't you rather a little inconvenience than the possibility of corrupted elections? Free and fair elections are the foundation of Democracy.

"If a political party does not have the foundation in the determination to advance a cause that is right and that is moral, then it is not a political party; it is merely a conspiracy to seize power." - Dwight D. Eisenhower

"He [President Biden] adopted the Bernie Sanders prescription for America...The President signed up for Bernie Sander's agenda to turn America into a Socialist country... and they've hit a brick wall, the reason they've hit a brick wall is that the American people are not in favor of it.

"If I were the President I'd listen to the American People, and I would pivot and try to become the moderate I said I would be... if he does that there are many Republicans' including myself who are willing to talk to him about making progress on the country like we did on Infrastructure." (Senator Mitch McConnel R- Ky [Minority Leader])

"I don't know why the activists are so upset about Joe, because "moderate" Joe is dead. He's buried. What you saw up there is some guy that wants to Federalize elections." (Gutfeld)

"The Constitution sets out the powers of the Federal Government...and whatever was not listed was left to the states or the people, or the individual." (Trey Gowdy) In America, the House and the Senate, the Judiciary, and the Executive branches work together to balance each other out, it's called a "Checks and Balances" system. It prevents one branch from usurping power over another. Thus, in his push to Federalizing elections, the Congress denied President Biden from changing the Senate Filibuster Rule.

FAILED AND SUCCESSFUL SOCIALIST COUNTRIES

Failed Socialist Countries

The largest of the failed socialist countries is the Soviet Union, which fell in 1991. Following WWII, the United States helped rebuild Western European countries, all of whom were free marketing economies that rebuilt rapidly by establishing the European Union and trading with one another. On the other hand, the Soviet Union seized government control of Eastern European nations, all of which became socialist states. These included: Bulgaria, East Germany, Hungary, Poland, Romania, Czechoslovakia, Belarus, and Ukraine. While East Germany reunified with West Germany and joined the thriving EU economy, the rest of the Eastern European countries faced economic hardship after the Soviet Union fell. Many of these countries remain the poorest European countries today.

Additionally, both Cuba and Venezuela are currently socialist states facing their own economic crises deemed a result of socialism.

Some argue that there has been no completely socialist country that has been successful, only countries that have seen success in adopting socialist policies.

- Bolivia is an example of a prosperous socialist country. Bolivia has drastically cut extreme poverty and has the highest GDP growth rate in South America.

[Some] other countries that have adopted and enacted socialist ideas and policies to various degrees and have seen success in improving their societies by doing so, are Norway, Finland, Sweden, Denmark, Canada, the Netherlands, and Ireland.

Finland may be a good example of a combination between capitalism and socialism:

The best way to look at Finland's economy and politics may be to see it as a blend of capitalism and socialism. Some people refer to this a "compassionate capitalism," meaning that markets can run freely, with minimal government regulation and interference; the role of the government is to ensure the social welfare by providing generous benefits to the population through to revenue generated by taxes. Those benefits include free schools, including college, for all students and generous maternity and paternity leave for new parents... Finland's model may work so well because the country's population is relatively small and homogenous.

Is Canada a Socialist Country?

Canada has a free-market, capitalist economy, where both small businesses and corporation are flourishing. The tech and AI industries are growing rapidly in Canada, thanks to its business-friendly policies, and skilled workers are migrating there from other countries to contribute to its boom.

This boom would not be possible without an economic system that favors people who work hard, remain competitive and contribute to the financial success of the industry and the country.

There is probably no such thing as a truly socialist country, and Canada is a case in point. Though many American politicians point to Canada as a socialist success story, its system only contains elements of socialism to help close the gap between the wealthiest and the poorest.

Populations of Democratic Socialist Countries:

Norway	5,465, 630
Finland	5,548,360
Sweden	10,160,169
Denmark	5,813,298
Canada	38,246,108
Netherlands	17,173,099
Ireland	4,982,907

In Contrast:

USA	331,000,00

Since the United States has a population of over 331 million with such a diverse demographic of people, it would have trouble with this perfect harmony between capitalism and socialism like in Finland and it would not be sustainable. There are many differences between America and the smaller European countries. One of the major differences is the population. (See table above)

There are some socialist programs that work already in effect in the United States like Social Security, Disability SSI, Medicare, and Medicaid for the disabled and elderly, housing subsidies, Public Schools, Community Colleges, State Universities, Vocational Schools, and Apprenticeship Programs, substance abuse treatment and prevention programs, community support programs for people with mental disabilities like MBI, Green Door, and Community Connections, EBT food stamps, Transgender and LGBT community clinics and programs like Whitman Walker and HIPS, and many others. We cannot say that we have not gained some good parts from socialist policies of the past. Under President Roosevelt, Social Security established a promise that lasts to this day: "growing old would never again mean growing poor." Here in the USA, we have implemented socialist policies that have helped many people.

America is always working to better itself, and the people; the citizens of the United States, make the decisions on who they want to elect to govern at the particular moment in time. That is the beauty of America, we have the power of the people; the Presidents' boss IS the people. Every four years we have a choice who we want to elect as the peoples' representative for our country; our President.

THREE NATIONS THAT TRIED SOCIALISM AND REJECTED IT

Israel, India, and the United Kingdom all adopted socialism as an economic model following World War II.

Socialism is guilty of a fatal conceit: It believes its system can make better decisions for the people than they can for themselves.

Socialism has failed in every country in which it has been tried.

Socialists are fond of saying that socialism has never failed because it has never been tried. But in truth, socialism has failed in every country in which it has been tried, from the Soviet Union beginning a century ago to three modern countries that tried but ultimately rejected socialism—Israel, India, and the United Kingdom.

While there were major political differences between the totalitarian rule of the Soviets and the democratic politics of Israel, India, and the U.K., all three of the latter countries adhered to socialist principles, nationalizing their major industries, and placing economic decision-making in the hands of the government.

And yet, socialism still beguiled leading intellectuals and politicians of the West. They could not resist its siren song, of a world without strife because it was a world without private property. They were convinced that a bureaucracy could make more-informed decisions about the welfare of a people than the people themselves could. They believed, with John Maynard Keynes, that "the state is wise, and the market is stupid."

At first, socialism seemed to work in these vastly dissimilar countries. For the first two decades of its existence, Israel's economy grew at an annual rate of more than 10 percent, leading many to term Israel an "economic miracle." The average GDP growth rate of India from its founding in 1947 into the 1970s was 3.5 percent, placing India among the more prosperous developing nations. GDP growth in Great Britain averaged 3 percent from 1950 to 1965, along with a 40 percent rise in average real wages, enabling Britain to become one of the world's more affluent countries.

But the government planners were unable to keep pace with increasing population and overseas competition. After decades of ever declining economic growth and ever rising unemployment, all three countries abandoned socialism and turned toward capitalism and the free market.

The resulting prosperity in Israel, India, and the U.K. vindicated free marketers who had predicted that socialism would inevitably fail to deliver the goods. As British prime minister Margaret Thatcher observed, *"the problem with socialism is that you eventually run out of other people's money."*

The Crisis Situation

The Coronavirus is now a worldwide Pandemic. Now Democrats want to propose bills and legislation to gain more government control and raise the taxes on the people. They are offering permanent government growth for a temporary crisis. Best Democrat slogan: "Let no crisis go to waste" (Ingraham). It is a perfect opportunity to gain as much power as they can, while they can. When people are scared strike now! "It is better to reign in Hell than to serve in Heaven". And *"You cannot expect the Government to do everything for you… at some point you have to take care of yourself"* (Perino). Keep in mind "They [Socialists] are not creative, just controlling… they have not discovered the cure, but will take credit and use that to their advantage" (Gutfeld).

Socialists are not finding cures and vaccinations to this problem. It is the Free Market that will be finding the cures, the competition of Health Industries, and Innovation will play a big part. The head Democrats: Pelosi, Schumer, Biden/Harris want to offer as a solution more government **control** instead of new ideas; to **tell** you when we can open, to **tell** you when you will close, to **mandate** you to take the vaccine, to **mandate** you to wear a mask. *Do as I say, not as I do.* Is it a good idea that in times of crisis invite government to creep into your life?

It's about POWER and gaining more power for themselves, and taking it from you, the American People. Government creep.

"The thing about this Pandemic and everything dragged out is that the Left and democrats want to drag out this Pandemic and want people to be afraid for as long as possible because it gives them political power". (Smith)

"The Democrats are expert practitioners of the politics of fear"

"Democrats are relying on the vulnerability that they create to enact their agenda. Injecting fear and panic to push this multi trillion-dollar disaster."

Explain: "When you look at this grab bag of Socialist proposals, they are a pretty hard sell because they don't comport with either experience or reason, and the Democrats kind of deep down know that, and so what they rely on is the politics of fear. They are expert practitioners of the politics of fear; why? Because if you think about fear, it is fear of the unknown that causes you to suspend your reason and do things that you wouldn't normally otherwise do. Almost a century ago, FDR, a Democrat warned us about fear he said, *"The only thing you have to fear is fear itself"*

What he meant is that fear is kind of un-American, fear can paralyze you, fear can ultimately become the problem itself, but not for Democrats today, fear for them today is an opportunity.

And if you look at the Coronavirus is only the latest, I mean a generation ago they were talking about the Ozone layer, dissipating the earth, running out of food, next it was Climate Change. They are trying to introduce a hysteria because in the hysteria they want people to act in ways that they would never act if they gave it sober consideration...

Alexandria Ocasio-Cortez's chief of staff said a very revealing thing recently: *"You guys may look at this climate changing business as being about the climate, we don't, for us it's all about changing the economy"*. Here is a chance to do things by invoking climate. He couldn't care less whether the earth is getting hotter or colder, he doesn't know the science, he doesn't care, but it is a pretext for doing things that you could not otherwise do. The same thing here, the bunch of these Pelosi proposals have nothing to do with fighting the health crisis, they have nothing to do with jobs.

It is basically a way to push proposals they have been trying to get away with for a long time, but that met with the resistance of a kind of a "calm reason", and political good sense, and now they are hoping to shove them by because they think we're all too scared to do otherwise." (D'Souza)

"The world is going to end in 12 years if we don't address climate change." (Alexandria Ocasio-Cortez)

"I think this green approach to governing is a religion for the Democratic Party and they are pushing electric vehicles you see in Superbowl ads pushing pickup trucks that are electric; but the pickup drivers think they are crap, they have terrible range, they can't carry anything, but [Biden's] government is forcing our auto companies to make these things and this is part of the religion of climate change that Biden is too attached to give it up." (Fred Fleitz) There

are other ways to be an environmentalist, and love and care for the earth other than to push "climate change" and buy into the GREEN NEW DEAL, and all that it entails.

A study out of New York University finds now more people are voting Republican. "This study focused on voting, and in terms of society on the whole moving more toward liberal side, that's been decided in the courts. That's not really what you vote on, but what you vote on what people in this study care about and what is drawing the Left to vote Republican is: government oversight, health care, and the 2nd Amendment and others, and those fundamental bedrock issues of the Republican Party among others is crucial.

And especially the more we go the more we have presidents like Biden who are spending astronomical amounts, who are growing the Federal Government to astronomical sizes. And that is why people are voting Republican because they don't want the government regulating everything and forcing you to believe a certain way or act a certain way and the like." (Compagno)

In America, we do not need, or want our government telling us what to do, how to live, how to maintain our bodies and our health, and how to run our businesses or our property.

CULTURALLY SPEAKING

The Democrats of yesteryear were the party of the "NeoLiberal Order" from its emergence in the 1970's to its decline in the 2010's. The core beliefs of the Democrat party at that time were:

Free Communication
Free Capital
Free Information
Free Trade
Personal Freedom

While Republicans at that time believed in:

Respect for Family
Respect for the Divine
Defense of Country

And it was believed that they had a resistance to feminism, race issues and homosexuality.

When President Clinton was in office, after the Reagan years, he often met with Newt Gingrich, Speaker of the House from 1995-1999. While they were on opposite sides, Clinton being a Democrat, and Newt Gingrich being a Republican, they opposed each other politically, it was said they "hated" each other. But they did work together to sort out the Nation's problems.

During these meetings, they agreed on the core values of strong family and strong markets. That is how they were able to come together to discuss the issues of the day and move forward with policy making decisions for the Nation. They were able to do this in unison while presiding over one of the biggest economic booms in American history. *"These two power brokers worked together on legislation that would shape America's political economy for a generation."* (Gerstle)

Today, our politics is so polarized, you either are on one side or the other, and there is real hatred to the point of real nastiness. Although it's mostly the Left hating the Right. *"I have never been so discriminated against until I came out as a Republican."* (MT) The word unification was thrown around in Biden's campaign and Inaugural speech; however, there is no unification going on in the upper levels of our government today, nor in our society.

Many Democrats have severed relations with old friends, husbands, wives, moms, dads, family members, community members, and classmates because of being on the opposite sides of the political aisle. That is where we get the word 'cancel' as in Cancel Culture. It literally means that people are willing to throw their peers under a bus because they disagree politically. It can come as defamation of character, or stifling/ruination/ boycott of one's businesses or career. Its target is to silence one's right to speech and the right to assemble.

Sometimes, as radical as erasing people from certain communities, and businesses, and even fining an employee 100,000$ for a single tweet they disagree with.

This is an example of our most primal flaw as human beings, coming out in what we can call 'tribalism.' This is when people stick with persons only in their 'tribe;' people with whom they agree. The attitude is: 'Us or Them' - Democrat vs Republican. *"Seems to be that they pick lousy stances based on what we choose. If I decide I'm going to come out in favor of breathing, the democrats are going to say you know what- they are just going to stop breathing, and it's a weird petulant way to choose the things you believe in."* (Gutfeld) There is something called 'Trump Derangement Syndrome', that makes people go crazy on Trump and Republicans.

Cultural Marxism

What really is Marxism? According to Whitaker Chambers it is: *"The 2nd oldest religion known to man founded by the serpent who whispered to Eve "ye shall be as gods." It's a profound human force, a profound desire to believe that you know good and evil, and then to seek to define good and evil for others."* (Max Eden)

That is why so many people are being canceled. It is because people are labeling and deciding that other people are 'evil' because they voted for Donald Trump or are an 'evil' Republican because they have different views than you do. A human does not have the power to judge other human beings; but they are in our culture silencing, cancelling their political opponents, and 'unfriending' their once peers. *"Whoever says he is in the light, yet hates his brother, is still in the darkness."* (1 John 2:7-10)

"You're also seeing a generational change where Republicans are finally growing up, growing some courage and fighting back against the people who are hurting their voters and their values. This is such an important phase shift in America where Republicans seem to be growing a spine." (J.D. Vance)

The Latino Community

Latinos are soundly rejecting the Democratic Party since 2012 -2020. The Latina vote for Democrats is down 8%, and up 8% for Republicans. That's 16% more toward Republicans in the Latino Community. (Hilton)

Former Democratic Leader of the California Senate Gloria Romero says: "I don't think the Democratic Party is really listening. They have gone so far left that basically we, Latinos, don't recognize the party anymore. It has lost not only its moral compass, its lost basic common sense. It's too late for the Democrats to turn around what they have been doing these past couple of years.

For example: the economy, this economy is crushing us, we are seeing the loss of energy independence, gas prices are killing us.

Latinos are the fastest growing sector of the small business associations, as you mention as well, we believe in school choice, the woke-ism over "birthing people" when we, as Latino people, support and celebrate not only one Mother's Day, but we have two Mother's Days.

Across the country whether we be Cuban American in Florida, or Mexican American in Nevada or here in California, we are seeing a tremendous shift in just saying 'Ya basta'- enough with a too woke party that's more interested in identity politics and has really forgotten what it was supposed to be and that is to really meet the needs of the poor, the oppressed, the minority, the working-class voters that we Latinas are. We also believe in citizenship; we are a very patriotic community, and we see the demise of the so called "defund the police". Did you know here in Los Angeles 50% of the lives that were hurt with crime were Latinos? We don't believe in the defunding of the police that so many of the Far -Left Democrats have been calling for. They've lost us. We very much believe in the American Dream, in having an opportunity of course we'd like to see a fair comprehensive immigration reform, but we value citizenship, we believe in this country.

If you take a look at the war death after any war, you will find the names Rodriguez, Gonzales, Romero so many names who have stepped up to serve this country, and that's the way it's going to be. At this point I'd say basically the Latinos are free agents. The question will be is: will the Republican Party step up and offer us as well a fair platform for us to continue this mass exodus out of the Democrat ranks?" (Gloria Romero)

Voice of Sergio Gomez, Restaurateur

"They have a lot of Latinos in Congress; the power is there but they don't do anything."

"This country has two faces. I can show you one face now, I want you to see, but when I'm with you I show another face."

"When I got amnesty, it was Republican it was Ronald Reagan, but he was different, he was real. He was Mexican American, he has more Latino heart, but Biden is not going to do anything about the Latinos, he is a white boy."

"We cannot force to them to come in without permission what Latino does they have the warning, but they're wrong. You know how much supplies you have in your house, but I'm coming in with my family too."

"People are here already, they are paying taxes, been here 25 years and they've been paying taxes, but have no paperwork, like the Dreamers. How can you make plans to buy property when you might have to go back? You do not have a permit; you need a license. The Democracy has to work on that."

"You can't be arrested 5 times; you have to be eligible. There has to be a system to choose or decide if they are eligible. Now it's a problem because everybody does what they want. Balance, for the good people, go to school, be a good student, bad one sends to therapy."

"There are some they think they come to America and get all the things, food stamps they want to live for free honey, they never want to work back home".

"In El Salvador people are OK, we have no problem. Nicaragua is like Cuba and Venezuela, but people from other countries just want to have fun."

"Cuba is like a slave."

"Give money to a country and does not supervise the money and the politicians get mansions and the people go hungry and die, but USA do that to look good."

"The black people get paid food stamps; they take care of your rent. That happens to real Americans because they have papers. Why they support people who never want to work they have rent paid and collect money? We have to work, but have no privilege, they do not work and have privilege."

"Not everyone is the same it's not all the Latinos is the same, not all black people the same, not all white people the same."

"To Politicians the more confused the better for them. Whoever talks nice is a liar."

"Sometimes the men come gets the woman pregnant, then leaves, that's when the foods stamps come."

"Parents pay people (Coyotes) to cross the border then they have to own them and pay more money because the politics in this country is nothing serious, only fantasy."

"They give too much to the person not permitted. We have to work to survive. It is not easy in this country." (Gomez)

"You need laws. Executive orders come and go. When you have law, and the law has been tested in court and constitutionally, that is the only way. We need comprehensive immigration reform, or our hearts will keep breaking when terrible cases happen." (Geraldo)

The Black Community and BLM

"African Americans approve of President Biden 67% down from 20 point. Those words resonate and what Donald Trump was saying, there is an element of truth that some Democrats believe. I didn't vote for Donald Trump, but there are a number of African Americans who did. These numbers are alarming when we are headed into a season where Democrats are on the ballot in the House and the Senate." (Harold Ford, Jr)

The Black Lives Matter organization is now showing its true colors. While everybody agrees with the slogan that 'black lives matter', the organization has been fleecing the black community and accepting donations that have been used to buy multi-million-dollar mansions. BLM leaders use 6 million dollars in donations to buy a massive, beautiful California mansion.

"After summer of 2020 we'd heard that Black Lives Matter took in, I think, 90 Million Dollars and we wondered what they were going to spend their money on, now we know they've spent 6 million dollars on a mansion for themselves" *"They use black Americans for profit, ever since George Floyd's death Black Lives Matter has profited from George Floyd's death, what have they done for the black community? Where are the Community Centers? Where is the improvement in education? They used this money for personal gain, and you look at that house, that house does not help black America, it is basically blood money, and it is sickening and is embarrassing black Americans were exploited for the personal gain of a few."* (Leo Terrell)

"Anyone that is surprised by BLM's shady shenanigans hasn't been paying attention. There are so many of us that have been screaming for years they are not really for black people. Any organization that seeks to destroy the nuclear family has no idea how important that is to the community, and they just don't care. I've said for years that the only way BLM really cares about straight black men is when they are dead. So, of course everybody should be asking where's the money? Show me the money." (Shemeka Michelle) Black Lives Matter, the organization, is a Marxist organization. "This is so very very sad because so many people believe in the Black Lives Matter, the Movement, it was the organization that was hateful, it was the organization that said give us your money or we'll bring your corporation or business down." (Judge Jeanine Pirro)

Unfortunately this behavior mimics Putin's ownership of a 700-million-dollar yacht, the fleecing of his people for his own gain.

"Black Lives Matter was a pseudo radical movement that exploited the suffering, and the irony is that it did nothing to save black lives. The majority of black males are killed by black males, never once in the entire tenure of this ideological movement was there any real discussion of how black people are being subjected to criminal behaviors when it is tacitly endorsed, and the politicization to suggest that we should abolish or defund police is suicidal.

At best the black churches and clear-thinking black folks must now build a movement of faith that is going to put boots on the ground to do what the Black Lives Matter failed to do with millions of dollars, none of which has been accounted for, none." (Reverend Eugene Rivers III) It is easy to post up catchy phrases, it is hard to tackle real problems.

Voice of a Black Woman, Sierra

How does it feel being a black woman in America, do you feel you have an equal opportunity for advancement?

"I think it depends not so much on race as it does on your background, your family. It's your family and your education and your family's wealth. If you come from a family that has money, it's easier to advance because you can get the education, and wealthy families have a better network and connections."

What do you think about the nuclear family in black communities? A Mom and Dad and children being the nuclear family?

"It's rare in families, its more single Dads and single Moms and single Grandparents."

What do you think of the BLM movement?

"I think it's a cult, it's a bunch of witches. I think they practice black magic. It has nothing to do with black lives and has everything to do with witchcraft and rituals."

Do you feel anger at our country because of our history? How do you think we can heal the wounds of our past?

I'm not so angry at the country itself. I'm angry about the amount of mass murders in so many different forms. If you are working and have a birth certificate and social security card, you're livestock. You got millions and millions of abortions every year and all these man-made diseases, and bringing them into this country, and the vaccinations they are putting in your body starting as a child.

Do you think we get along today? How are race relations?

No, because we trained to hate each other; the movies, and the separate communities, its designed for us to hate each other. They treat foreigners better that actual Americans. If you come into this country, you get loans for businesses, and loans for houses, scholarships, and when Africans come over, they think they are better us, white and black. They see so much negative stuff on the television in movies and on the news, they stereotype us, think we are lazy, our ancestors already worked for our country, they are getting everything Chinese, Italians, Africans, Korean are the main ones. I don't know if its China or Korean, but they're the ones who own the shops in my neighborhood.

As a black woman what do you feel is the most important belief, value to you?

My relationship with my Creator. My faith that's all I got, because if they take away everything; my children, house, cars, they can't take away my faith. My faith- based spirituality.

Who is your favorite black American figure?

Harriet Tubman because she helped free many of slaves.

What is the biggest problem facing the black community in 2022?

Who we are, our identity, who we are as a black people, we don't even know who we are our identity, our history.

As a woman, what do you think of transgenders in women's sports?

I think it is unfair to other women to compete against a man, a biological man shouldn't compete against a woman. It should be against the law. It should be illegal. If you put a man on a woman's basketball team, it's no longer a woman's basketball team.

What do you think of all the border crossings?

You mean people from foreign countries sneaking into this country? I feel like they are doing nothing more than what Columbus did, take over the country from the Indians.

Do you know what socialism is?

I have no idea what it is. I have no idea what socialism is. I feel like that is a new word. I didn't start hearing about socialism until a few years ago.

Do you want to see it in America?
I heard it already is a part of America.

Voice of a Black Man, Malcolm

As a black man in America do you feel like you have an equal opportunity for advancement? Do you believe in the American Dream?

I had lost hope a long time ago. I didn't think that anything can be equal, but now, if you have some get up and go about yourself you can accomplish some things you want to accomplish. It still tricky, no matter what its always going to be racism in the country and in the world. Different people have different ideas of what their American Dream is; for some it's to get what you need, for some it's the house and the white picket fence.

What do you feel about the nuclear family? Or what are you able to do for your family?

My immediate family? I'm able to educate them as far as life and things going on in the world more so educating about things.

What do you think about the Black Lives Matter movement/organization?

I think is tremendously good especially if it's for a good cause, and it is not for one person's gain, but if it's for a good cause I am for that.

Do you feel anger about our country's history and how can we heal our wounds from the past?

The thought will always be there. I would get angry about the past, me as a human being quite naturally get angry, but each one has to love one another.

As a black man, what is your most important belief or value to you?

Number 1 is my Higher Power. That's my most and foremost, 2nd is my family. My family is everything to me. I have 4 boys, and 1 girl, 3 grandchildren.

And are you still together with the mom or Grandmom?
One of my sons; his mom and I are together.

Who is your favorite black American figure?
I respect Malcolm X, I would say.

What is the biggest problem facing the black community in 2022?
The Opioid epidemic, drugs, and the police.

How do you feel about the LGBT community? And Transgender in woman's sports?

My thing is they got a life also. What they do doesn't affect me one wit or another, they are human being also, they're human.

What do you think of all the people coming across the border?

I feel a lot of people are searching for the America Dream. I guess that is what people are looking for. It doesn't bother me, there were people here before me, people have always been looking for a new way of life. If they are bringing something negative, we don't need anything negative.

What do you think about guns?

I still like guns. I really do. If it's for a cause, and it's not harming someone as malice, then I'm for it. People can protect themselves and their homes.

What do you hope to teach or leave behind for the younger generation?

—Knowledge

—Wisdom

—Understanding

Do you know what socialism is? And do you want to see it in this country?

I'm not really into socialism. I don't know how to define it. I know what being social is, but I don't know.

War on Cops

Deaths of police officers has gone up from 46 in 2020 to 73 in 2021. That is a 56% increase.

"Violence against law enforcement in this country is one of the biggest phenomenon's that doesn't get enough attention. Last year officers were being killed at a rate of 1 in every 5 days. An almost alarming percentage of the 73 law enforcement officers killed in the line of duty last year were killed through things like being ambushed. They were killed for being police officers. Wearing the badge shouldn't make you a target." (Christopher Wray)

Voice of a Native American, Savannah

Do you, as a Native American, believe you have an equal opportunity for advancement in this country?

I think it depends, my family came from a disadvantaged position, that I'm not sure if it was our race in particular. We did grow up in poverty, my dad did, he is fully Native American. It's more a class thing, in the Native American Community it is a lot more difficult to achieve the higher class on Reservations than off the Reservation.

Do you believe in the American Dream, and do you think all people can strive for it?

I don't think all people can. I think it is a dream for people who were born in upper/middle class, not so much in a lower- class position because we don't have the same access to things like water quality, health care, mental health care, and education on Reservations, it is not like an area like DC.

America is very Eurocentric, a lot of it is based on Eurocentric families, like in movies.

What is your priority now in your life?

Just to be happy.

Do you feel an attachment to your people/ your ancestors?

I would say so, yeah. I am very interested in learning about my culture.

What tribe are you from?

Blackfoot.

What would you like to see for the Native American Community?

I would like to see them get more funding from the government, because the land is land, they stole from them. They need access to better health care, mental health care, rehabilitation programs; there is a lot of Alcoholism on Reservations.

What do you think about the Washington Football team's old name? The Redskins?

I'm not a huge fan of the old mascot. I'm glad they changed it. I think if someone, like a huge NFL team, should have that logo they should give back to the Indigenous Community.

Would you like to see an Indigenous People's Day?

Yeah

What is the biggest issue facing the Native American community in 2022?

The ongoing issues of our Reservations are not being well funded or taken care of and it's been like that for a long time/decades.

What do you think about the people crossing the border?

Its good, they should. America was built from Immigrants, and Immigrants continue to build this country. Immigrants from all over have brought great things here.

What do you think of Transgenders in woman's sports?

I think they should be allowed.

Do you follow American Politics?

As much as I can, yeah.

Do you know what socialism is? And do you want to see it in America?

I don't have the best understanding of socialism, but its more what I align with. I'd like to see more new ideas from both sides being brought to the table.

Do you feel like you are American? Do you feel patriotic to this country of what it is today?

I feel like ethnically, I am American. As patriotically, I'd say no because I don't support all of what big politicians are saying.

What would you like to see in America?

Am really terrified of Row vs. Wade being overturned. I think more women's rights should be respected. We all have to be kind to each other.

Voice of an Immigrant, Funmilay Ogunbiya

As an Immigrant, do you feel you have an equal opportunity for advancement in this country?

Yes

What do you feel was/is your biggest struggle?

Nothing

Do you believe Immigrants believe in the American Dream, and can they achieve it?

Yeah, believe, but not everybody. Some people come here for visiting/ students, but that does not apply to me, I am a citizen.

I came here through the Lottery.

Do you believe Immigrants assimilate into US culture? Or do they keep cultures of back home?

No, because everybody respects their own culture. If they don't respect their culture how can they speak their own language, or dress?

Where are you from?

I am Nigerian, Africa.

How did you Immigrate to America?

I won the lottery.

Do you feel discriminated against?

Yes, when I was pregnant, they told me they cannot accept a pregnant woman working in the company. Once it showed, they stopped me working, they don't accept pregnant woman working. That is not my current job.

What do you think of the people crossing the border?

The people coming in don't care. To me it's a risk of life. They just want to cross anywhere, anyhow. I saw the woman throwing the baby to the other side, they don't care, it's a risk of life.

What do you think of Transgender Women in women's sports?

You know, I don't against anyone. I love them, I support them. I don't discriminate anyone.

What is the most important value to you?

My job, my late Father, and my children.

Is there anything you want to say that I did not ask?

I am ok.

Is your life better in America that it was in Africa?

YES - I have 7 brothers, and they depend on me. I am the bread-earner of my family.

Do you send money back home?

Yes, I send money back home. The opportunity we have in this country, we do not have back home. Here we pay taxes, we receive. Back home we pay taxes, we don't receive. Here we have free health insurance, I have Medicaid for low income, you have a lot of benefits for the children. Children go to school for free, but back home it's not like that. Here we get free phone, free tablets, back home no. Here you receive SSI or SSDI (Social Security Insurance, or Social Security Disability Insurance). Here you can talk, back home children cannot talk to Elders, they are limited to say "yes" or "no." Whatever your husband say is final in Africa.

Do you know what socialism is? And would you like to see it in this country?

Mmm. I don't know what to say about that. I don't like it. I don't practice it. I like to be alone. (Ogunbiya)

The LGBT Community

Voice of a Transgender Woman, A.S.

As a transgender Woman, do you feel you have an equal opportunity for advancement in this country?

I don't, but I came from a different era, transgenders have more opportunities now than what I had growing up.

What do you feel was/is your biggest struggle?

Fitting in comfortably, being unsafe in situations feeling someone could be upset because I am Trans.

Do you feel gender should be taught to kindergartners? Five-year old's- to 2nd graders?

NO

What do you feel about the Disney World coming out to say, "dreamers of all ages" instead of "boys and girls?"

Cis gender and all that is new wording. I didn't mind it saying: "boys and girls," I like the distinction, for me I feel like wanted to be a girl.

What do you feel is the biggest issue facing Transgenders today?

Over saturation. I don't like the forcing. You can't get the people on your side by forcing people to accept you. There only certain groups of people that matter, your family and friends.

When I was coming through, I didn't care if everyone accepted me. Respect and pro-nouns: if I represent as a female, call me she, it's about respect in my presence, or call me by my name. I find it ridiculous that inanimate objects can be 'she' like boats and cars, but people refuse to call people by their appropriate pronouns.

Do you feel discriminated against?

Often times, often fear for my safety. I'm pretty passable, so It's more when men hit on me, and I tell them I am Trans. I don't want to be murdered because someone finds out I am trans.

Do you think Transgender Women should be in woman's sports?

I think it should be case by case. I don't think someone who started hormones at 25 should play against a woman. But like Native Americans have that 3rd gender; Transgender is a qualifier, Male/Female/Trans. You can't just decide that you're a girl because you're losing in men's sports. I started transitioning before puberty, so I started estrogen very young at 14, that is way different than 17. They were athletes before their transitions, so they have a lot of muscles.

What would you like to see for the Transgender community going forward?

A world where Transgender people can live and be ourselves. Gender is a social thing, but sex is a biology thing. Gender and sex are different. That's the reason why you have to "transition."

You see videos of someone saying, "yes sir" and she came back and says, "ITS MA'AM!!!" Come on, please look the part that you're trying to be...

What do you think of the people crossing the border?

I definitely think there should be a system. Like if it's done the right way.

What's the most important belief, or value to you?

My Higher Power

Do you think Transgender Women should be in women's prisons?

Only if they've had sex changes.

Do you believe in the American Dream?

I want the dream of to be who I want to be.

Do you know what socialism is? And would you like to see it in our country?

I kind of know what socialism is, explain it to me. (AS)

The Log Cabin Republicans

Log Cabin Republicans is the nation's original and largest organization representing LGBT conservatives and straight allies who support fairness, freedom, and equality for all Americans.

Log Cabin Republicans has state and local chapters nationwide, full-time staff in Washington, DC, a federal political action committee, and state political action committees. There are over 80 chapters nationwide.

The name of the organization is a reference to the first Republican President of the United States, Abraham Lincoln, who was born in a Log Cabin. President Lincoln built the Republican Party on the principles of liberty and equality under the law. The party should return to its roots. When the organization was founded, the name, "Lincoln Club", was already taken by another GOP group, so organizers instead chose the name Log Cabin Republicans.

Log Cabin Republicans got its start in California during the late 1970's mainly about gay teachers. The DC Chapter came in the 90's with Rich Tafel. Log Cabin Republicans are LGBT Republicans and straight allies who support equality under the law for all, free markets, individual liberty, limited government, and a strong national defense.

"The cause is righteous. Despite all the drama, we all have a purpose to support a cause that is bigger than ourselves." (AW)

Voice of a Gay Man, Adam Savit, (President of Log Cabin Republicans, DC Chapter)

I came on 5 years ago; it was already a DC chapter and already had social initiatives planned.

Do you feel a person in the LGBT community has an equal opportunity here in America for advancement?

Yes

What trends have you seen through different presidencies? What did you see when Trump was in office? Now Biden?

There was a huge transition, very pro Trump message, but it was still divided. In 2019 LCR endorsed Trump, the majority voted to endorse Trump. It was a huge transformation, we had a President who was pro- gay, pro- gay marriage and a Republican who wanted to work with us! By 2020 we were involved in Trump's campaign.

When did you see girls, lesbians/bi, joining the group, and why did they join?

There are not many, wish there were. I hope it could be a place for any gender who feels the Left doesn't tolerate them for their views. Some came because they had been cancelled from their lesbian communities because they didn't match the "lesbian democrat ideologue" thinking.

Have you seen the Log Cabin Republicans grow throughout the years?

Oh yeah, not to pat myself on the back, but 5 years ago 60 members now we are over 100 members. Meetings have gotten much bigger it's on average to see 50 members and non- members at the monthly meetings.

Have you been seeing more LGBT Republicans in leading positions in the government? And can you name them?

Former Ambassador to Germany Ric Grenell, he was the first gay anything in the Cabinet, not Pete Buttigieg. There are tons now, I can't think of local officials, there are some running.

What is your stance on family and gay marriage?

Yeah, I was kinda skeptical of gay marriage. I was more for domestic partners benefits. Now its settled and has legal recognition. Republicans are just as supportive as Democrats. At this point we are legally equal. Democrats are now trying to add their radical "pet" issues.

What do you think of Transgender in woman's sports?

I think it's very clear if you have a male born body that has gone through puberty and has all these male muscles then you should not compete against women.

What political issue is most important to LCR?

To make a space, a place where people like us can organize and socialize. It's a place where we can go.

Do you think the Republican Party has become more accepting of diversity in recent years?

Yes, no question.

Do you know what socialism is? And do you want to see it in America?

Yeah, I know what it is, and no I would not like to see it in America. Its more government control over resources and power.

Being a Republican, what are the issues/ values you most care about in 2022?

Economy, it is a disaster, inflation, energy prices. There are basic easy solutions for this, just getting government off of people's backs.

Would you say the Republican Party has shifted from its old roots of resisting Feminism, Race Issues, and Homosexuality to today's Republican Party?

Absolutely, in all meaningful ways we are done on all those issues. Just that when gays have marriage equality, and job security, and minorities have equal access to schools and jobs. I'm not interested in affirmative action. Dems are going into some crazy world with that. The Republican Party has come far on those issues. (Savit)

The Cultural Shift

America has bent more to the liberal side culturally, but now you are seeing a much stronger and more accepting Republican Party.

"Conservatism, in the classical sense, signifies respect for tradition, deference to existing institutions and the hierarchies that structure them, and are suspicious of change." (Gerstle) "The coming apart of the neoliberal order opened up space for Trump- style authoritarianism and Sanders- style socialism to flourish." (Gerstle)

The Democrats of today are not the Democrats of your Father's and Grandfather's generation anymore. The current Democrat Party is now a Bernie Sander's- style **socialist democratic party.** It is in many ways prevalent in today's society as I have laid out throughout this paper, in power grabs, silencing of political opponents, growth of government, passing off one narrative as the "truth" in our news, and using fear and real authoritarianism to govern all, head into one direction: a less free, **socialist state.** People may be concerned and label Trump as an "authoritarian" figure, but that is furthest from the truth. He may be boisterous and outspoken, but while statues were falling, our history was being "erased", and cities were being looted and burned in the summer of 2020, it was President Trump who came out in favor of our Founding Fathers.

He made a point to spend the Fourth of July 2020 at South Dakota's Mt. Rushmore. He loves the constitutionally grounded Institutions of America that give the power back to the *people.* Voting Republican is a much safer avenue to follow than to follow the path of the socialist.

Socialism is on the Move

In America, 2022, we are living Bernie Sanders vision. It is beginning; with high prices, controlling your mode of transportation (pushing electric vehicles), and large government. The new 'liberal world order' in the West is the implementation of the Green New Deal; changing democratic countries into socialist ones. *"We cannot move forward to a post carbon world without a shift to a socialist system."* (Landis) It has begun here in the U.S. under the Biden Administration and is happening elsewhere, now in particular, the Netherlands. The Dutch government is actively trying to seize farmer's land for their globalist green vision to use for collective (state) land. The farmers are fighting back.

Now people need to stand up and fight for their freedoms or else there will be no freedoms to fight for anymore! If the U.S. falls, the Western world will follow. China and Russia are just waiting in the wings. They need not press 'Climate Change' because they are already communist countries, and interestingly they do not care about emissions, pollution, or the global environment at all. China is the world's worst polluter and leads in CO_2 emissions by over 50%. They are patiently waiting for the U.S. to screw ourselves up, give up our Democracy, give up our Constitution, give up our Republic, all in fear of this thing called 'climate change'. It is a ruse. *"There is no Unity, Jow Biden doesn't want Unity. What Joe Biden wants is for every American to bend the knee to his agenda".* (Representative Byron Donalds)

"The credo here is 'Big Government Socialism', they want to transform the economy away from the principles of Free Market Capitalism and institute a kind of regulatory government planning socialist state, which emphasizes re-distribution and income leveling, not growth, not prosperity." (Kudlow)

In Conclusion

If you love your country, if you believe the words you utter in "The Pledge of Allegiance", if you feel pride when you look at the red, white, and blue, then don't vote for a Socialist! If you love all the beautiful people and communities, we have in this land you can see all the wonderful ideas, benefits, success, and happiness that Capitalism and a Free-Market Economy can bring to every community! *"You have a freer life if you are a capitalist!"* (Gutfeld). You can do anything, even if you don't achieve lots of wealth, stardom, or fame, your pursuits can be your own. Let them be your own! Be proud to let them be your own! Be proud to be an AMERICAN! Be glad that we can CHOOSE our paths.

And Reagan, I hope you in your life, when it comes down to making political decisions, you will elect to keep America America. And to not change it to what other people's *false promises of utopia's* are, which have oppressed, killed, and starved millions of people, because once America is gone it is GONE! It is better to take responsibility for your own life! Be Independent! Have a mind of your own! I do know America is not perfect, we've got to work on some things, take it upon yourselves: the youth of America, to make it an even better place to live! What will you create? How will you help shape and grow your communities? What will you contribute?

I do know from my years of studying History, and from the witnessing current events of today, I know it to be true that America with all its faults is the best place to be, to live, to grow, and to become your own person. *"It's time to embrace capitalism, not to abandon the values that make America the envy of the world."* (Haley) In this life, be smart.

Be compassionate. Be careful. The future is in your hands, and your generation's. God Bless the USA! To keep on keepin' ON!

THE END FOR NOW
Love,
Your Aunt Kitty

SOURCES

Preface/Socialism/Karl Marx:

"If you don't know a word, look it up on your phone." (**Anne Wake, Ph.D.**).

"I am not bound to win, but I am bound to be true. I am not bound to success, but I am bound to live up to what light I have inside me." (**Abraham Lincoln**).

Socialism Definition- (**Merriam-Webster**).

Similar and Opposite words - (**Oxford Languages**).

"Individual Liberty" (**Mark Levine** on **Life, Liberty, and Levine,** January 16th, 2022).

Antonyms: freedom, democracy, self-governance, republic, free enterprise, capitalism, liberty, human rights, free world, rule of law." (**Art Harman's Review**).

"A political and economic theory of social organization which advocates that the means of production, distribution, and exchange should be owned or regulated by the community as a whole." (*Oxford Dictionaries*- from **MBN -Market Business News,** January 17th, 2022).

"Policy or practice based on the political and economic theory of socialism. (In Marxist theory) a transitional social state between the overthrow of capitalism and the realization of Communism." (*Oxford Dictionaries*- from **MBN, Market Business News,** January 17th, 2022).

Karl Marx- Marx (1818-1883) was a philosopher, author, social theorist, and an economist. He is famous for his theories about capitalism and communism. (**Investopedia**).

Karl Marx, in full **Karl Heinrich Marx…**Marx and Engels form the basis of the body of thought and belief known as Marxism. (**Brittanica**-By **David T. McLellan**- updated January 5, 2022).

"See equality of wages as the goal of social revolution…"(**Karl Marx, Economic and Philosophic Manuscripts of 1844** found in bibliography in **The Life and Legacy of Karl Marx, The Fathers of Socialism** by **Charles River Editors-written,** 15 November 2020).

Karl Marx- Is best remembered for advocating socialism… (**The Life and Legacy of Karl Marx, The Fathers of Socialism** by **Charles River Editors-written,** 15 November 2020).

"With these measure in place, in the hands of the state, it will sweep away the conditions for the existence of class antagonism. And the proletariat will thereby abolish its own supremacy as a class." (**Karl Marx, The Life and Legacy of Karl Marx, The Fathers of Socialism** by **Charles River Editors-written,** 15 November 2020).

"Power tends to corrupt, and absolute power corrupts absolutely" (**Lord Acton** stated in a letter written to Bishop Mandell in 1887) (Lord Acton) (https://www.phrases.org.uk/).

Cuba has had a socialist political system since 1959 based on the "one state-one party" principle. Cuba is constitutionally defined as a Marxist-Leninist socialist state guided in part by the political ideas of Karl Marx and headed by Fidel Castro who died in 2016. (Wikipedia, 2020).

History of Russia:

The Soviet Union (USSR)- is a former norther Eurasian empire (1917/22-1991) stretching from the Baltic and Black seas to the Pacific Ocean and, in its final years, consisting of 15 Soviet Socialist Republics – (**Brittanica.com**- By **Richard E. Pipes**).

"In post-revolutionary Russia…to state run collective farms"- (USSR Established – Author:HISTORY.com Editors-Website: HISTORY= https://www.history.com/this-day-in-history/ussr-established last updated December 20th, 2021 Original published date: November 24th, 2009).

Vladimir Lenin, also called Vladimir Ilish Lenin… which became the Communist worldview"- (**Brittanica.com** By **Albert Resis**).

"Bolsheviks armed with guns ride in a truck in Vladivostok, Russia, in 1920. Led by Vladimir Lenin, the left-wing Bolshevik regime sought to silence its enemies through a state-sanctioned policy of mass killings and detainments known as the Red Terror."-Photograph by Cody Marsh. **NAT GEO IMAGE COLLECTION – How the red Terror set a macabre course for the Soviet Union- By Erin Blakemore-** Published September 2nd, 2020).

"The Red Terror was a Bolshevik-ordered campaign…and threats to Bolshevik power" (alphahistory.com- Alpha **History**).

Joseph Stalin Born: December 6, 1878, December 18, 1878, Gori Georgia **Died**: March 5th, 1953 (aged 74) Moscow (**Brittanica.com**-By **Ronald Francis Hingley**- last updated December 2nd, 2021).

Stalin- "1901 The revolutionary Bandit… Stalin resumed editorship of PRAVDA, and 1934-39 Stalin's great Terror… Around 750,000 people are summarily killed."- (**BBC TEACH**= Joseph **Stalin: National hero or cold-blooded murderer?**).

"I'll make the argument that these matters shouldn't be seen as discreet episodes, but seen together," said Naimark, the Robert and Florence McDonnell Professor of Eastern European Studies and a respected authority on the Soviet Regime. *"It's a horrific case of genocide- the purposeful elimination of all or part of a social group, a political group."* (Naimark) (Interview -By **Cynthia Haven**- Stanford Report, September 23rd, 2010) **Stalin Killed Millions. A Stanford historian answers the question, was it genocide?** Also: "The past few decades have seen terrifying examples in Rwanda, Cambodia, Darfur, and Bosnia."

Also: "Mass killing is still the way a lot of governments do business." (Historian **Norman Naimark** excepts, quotes and philosophies from his book "**Stalin's Genocides**").

"If one includes the combatant deaths, and the deaths due to war-related famine and disease…—perhaps about 20 million." (**China File-NYRB China Archive**- Feb 5th, 2018, **by Ian Johnson – Who Killed More Stalin, Hitler, or Mao?**).

Russia Today:

"Russia ranks 11th in the world… (**How big is the Russian Economy? Politifact-** Poynter Institute "**Russia's economy and Western sanctions - what you need to know**" Article: **by Louis Jacobson**, February 25th, 2022).

"To justify invading Ukraine, Vladimir Putin paints Russia… with a (GDP) not much larger than the state of Ohio's" (**The Russian economy is headed for collapse** by: **Eric Werker**- published: March 10, 2022, 10.20am EST- The conversation- **theconversation.com**).

"[Putin] *said it before the war, that Ukraine is not a nation…* (**Elana**- a Ukrainian Mom on **Cavuto Live,** March 19th, 2022).

[Putin is] an "authoritarian dictator" (**Steve Hilton** on **The Next revolution with Steve Hilton**, March 20th, 2022).

"Soviet style KGB cold blooded killer." (**Rebekah Koffler** on **The Next Revolution with Steve Hilton,** February 20th, 2022).

"It is fake news, it's not the truth, it is what the government wants you to believe." (**A Russian teen** on **Cavuto Live**, March 19th, 2022).

"This is suspected to be Vladimir Putin's 700-million-dollar yacht…" (**Harris Faulkner** on **The Faulkner Focus,** March 24th, 2022).

"His yacht game is strong… I wonder how this works out, is there a waiting list? Does everyone get a turn, do you book a family? Graduations? Proms?" (**Tyrus** on **Gutfeld!** March 24th, 2022) *'700 million dollars, that's almost a billion!'* (**Greg Gutfeld** on **Gutfeld!** March 24th, 2022).

"This is authoritarianism, this is a dictatorship, this is communism, this is socialism…" (**Pete Hegseth** on **The Faulkner Focus,** March 24th, 2022).

History of China:

"In the case of China, socialism is not only about equality. It is supposed to take the country towards an ultimate goal – Communism…" (Inkstone- **Is China Socialist? A long (and Better) answer**- By: **Alan Wong and Viola Zhou**, August 27th, 2018).

"On October 1, 1949, Chinese Communist leader Mao Zedong… United States to suspend diplomatic ties with the PRC for decades." (**Department of State; Office of the HISTORIAN**).

Mao Zedong:

"Mao Zedong, The Leader of the People's Republic of China… in what the Chinese Rural community rural community had suffered in recent history."- (**Mao's Great Leap Forward 'Killed 45 million in four years'**- By **Arifa Akbar,** *The Independent,* Friday, September 17th, 2010).

(**How to be a Dictator -The Cult of Personality in the Twentieth Century:** Author **Frank Dikötter**)

Mao's Great Famine: The Story of China's Most Devastating Catastrophe – (Author **Frank Dikötter**)

Communist China Today:

"Multiple media and NGOs estimated that since April 2017… The Church of Almighty God reported authorities subjected hundreds of their members to "torture or forced indoctrination." (CHINA (INCLUDES TIBET, XINJIANG, HONG KONG, AND MACAU) **2018 INTERNATIONAL RELIGIOUS FREEDOM REPORT**).

[Suppression of freedom in Hong Kong] (**The Hongkongermovie.com, The Acton Institute**).

"Torture of political opponents" (**Dan Bongino** on **Fox and Friends Saturday**, June 11th, 2022).

"The first thing that authoritarians try to do is to delegitimize and ban Religion because it is an existential threat against the state." (**Rachel Campos- Duffy on Fox and Friends,** July 15th, 2022).

"China has been destabilizing our economy for decades…" (**Steve Hilton** on **The Next Revolution,** January 30th, 2022).

"They need to understand the CCP does not represent all of the big core values of excellence…" (**Enes Kanter Freedom**- NBA Player- on **The Story with Martha MacCallum,** February 2nd, 2022).

History of Nazi Germany:

Nazi Party- political Party, Germany
"**Nazi Party**, byname of **National Socialist German Workers' Party...
totalitarian** methods until 1945." (**Britannica.com Article** "Nazi
Party"- Introduction).

*"The Nazi Party was founded as the German Workers' Party by Anton
Drexler... Hitler had ousted the party's other leaders and taken over."*
(**Britannica.com Article** "Nazi Party- **Founding of the Nazi Party
and the Beer Hall Putsch**).

In 1925, Adolf Hitler wrote in Mein Kampf..." (**Breeding the New
German "Race"-Holocaust and Human Behavior- www.facing
history.org-** Chapter 5). (I visited January 18th, 2022).

*"However, it was the effects of the Great Depression...Hitler in effect assumed
dictatorial powers."* (**Britannica.com Article "Nazi Party" -The Nazi
Party and Hitler's Rise to power**).

*"On July 14, 1933... Germany's Jews were effectively erased from public
life."* (**Britannica.com** Article "Nazi Party" -**The Nazi Party and the
Third Reich**).

*"When Germany started World War II... Therein Nazism imitated
communism."* (**Britannica.com** Article "Nazi Party" - **The Nazi Party
in World War II**).

"The outbreak of war also saw the full...of starvation or disease" (**Britannica.
com** Article "Nazi Party" - **The Nazi Party in World War II**).

*"The word "Holocaust," from the Greek words "holos" ... More than one
million of those who perished were children."* (**HISTORY.COM
EDITORS "The Holocaust"**).

Venezuela:

Nicolás Maduro- President of Venezuela
Candidate for the **United Socialist Party**
Nicolás Maduro, in full **Nicolás Maduro Moros** (born November 23,
1962, Caracas, Venezuela led to repeated attempts by the opposition
to remove him from office." "When Chávez died on March 5,

2013 (**BRITANNICA NICOLAS MADURO** BY: **Jeff Wallenfeldt-** Last Updated: Nov 19ᵗʰ, 2021).

"The council said that according to its latest figures, Nicolás Maduro won the election by 1.49 percentage points, or fewer than 225,000 votes." **(Venezuela election final results show narrower victory for Nicolás Maduro- Belle News- Read Think Share).**

Despite U.S. sanctions, the country's worst economic crisis in history... **(The U.S. predicted his downfall, but Maduro strengthens his grip on power in Venezuela, The Military Supports Maduro, and the plunging economy hasn't toppled Maduro** (By: **John Otis NPR NEWS 88.5 American University Radio-** Updated December 8, 20218:17 AM ET Heard on Morning Edition).

"Over the past 5 years, Venezuelans have seen their quality of life deteriorate to previously unthinkable levels..., refugees walk across mountainous terrain 700 km to Bogota, the capital and gateway to the rest of South America, or 500 km to Barranquilla, on the northern coast." **(TEARFUND- Connections- Stories from Venezuelan Refugees in Colombia -**March 2020).

The United States of America:

"The term "capitalism" was almost unknown in the English world until first popularized..." **City Press -Who Invented the Term 'Capitalism' and Why- news24.com).**

*"**Mercantilism** dominated the economic landscape in Europe during the sixteenth and seventeenth centuries."* **(Hillsdale College- The Development of Free Trade in Europe by: Gene A. King,** Jr -Oklahoma Baptist University).

"That capital is that of the commodity, as a useful object that may be exchanged on the market that stems from a need..." **(Karl Marx in Das Kapital, Volume 1** in **1867 -The Life and Legacy of Karl Marx, The Fathers of Socialism** by: **Charles River Editors, written** 15 November 2020).

Free Enterprise System -Definition **(Oxford Languages).**

"When people discuss the "free market," they mean an economy with unobstructed competition" -**(Investopedia).**

"In order for communism to truly thrive, you would have to be a minimalist. You can't be Madonna; you can't be a Material Girl." (**Reagan Templeton**, April 2nd, 2022).

*At the start of **2020**, numbers **just** over 331 million people (**Worldometer** population* estimation).

Also, since 2001, the share of federal income taxes paid by the top 1 percent increase from 33.2 percent to a new high of **40.1** percent in 2018.

In 2018, the top 50 percent of all taxpayers paid 97.1 percent of all individual income taxes, while the bottom 50 percent paid the remaining 2.9 percent. (**Tax Foundation -Summary of the Latest Federal Income Tax Data, 2021** Update by**: Erica York**, February 3rd, 2021).

The Entrepreneurial Spirit:

Entrepreneur Definition: (**Definitions from Oxford Languages**).

"The more you do, the more you can do. It's a snowball effect" (SDB) (**Sylvia Diane Beverly "Ladi Di"- The Love Poet**, March 31st, 2022).

"With work, tenacity, purpose, and patience" (words of **PS Perkins** P. S. Perkins, CEO, CCO **Human Communication Institute** (HCI)).

"Honesty, Integrity, and Hard Work. You can be honest every day, you can say what you are going to do and have the Integrity to do it…" (**Robert Moehling** on **YouTube** "Robert Is Here" tropical Fruit Market).

"The business of America is business." (**Calvin Coolidge**).

"Innovation is still Capitalism's Star. I think that America's business success through the decades has occurred because we have so many people with specialized knowledge who are willing to put their money, time, and resources on the line for ideas that can't be proved to a committee." (**New York Times** -Economic Review - **By Robert J. Shiller**, August 17th, 2013).

By assuming the autonomy of the individual, capitalism grants dignity to the poor. By affirming people's rights to their own labor, regardless of their position on the economic ladder, capitalism offers the poor the means to improve their well-being… As many in history have experienced, capitalism is the ideal economic system for the people around the world. Again, capitalism produces wealth and innovation, improves the lives of individuals, and gives power to the people. (**teenvogue.com**).

Two Stories:

President Dwight D Eisenhower: (**Three Days in January; Dwight Eisenhower's Final Mission**, by: **Bret Baier**, William Morrow, An Imprint of Harper Collins *Publishers,* 2017, p 15-20).

President Barack Obama: (**Barack Obama: Life Before the Presidency**, Consulting Editor: Michael Nelson, **millercenter.org**).

The Comparison Between Free Market and Socialism:

"Womb to Tomb"- (said esp. of care under the National Health Service. **WordReference.com**).

"Once government gets ahold of health care it's nothing but bureaucracy and red tape." (Aunt Bridget, April 1, 2022).

Representative Alexandria Ocasio-Cortez's proposal of the "GREEN NEW DEAL" on February 7th, 2019 ('**Representative Alexandria Ocasio-Cortez Releases Green New Deal Outline', NPR - All Things Considered,** article by: **Danielle Kurtzleben,** February 7th, 2019, 5:01 AM EST).

Infrastructure Investment and Jobs Act- 11/15/2021- Public Law No: 117-58 (for 1.85 Trillian dollars) passed. (H.R. 3684- Infrastructure Investment and Jobs Act, **Congress.gov, 117th Congress 2021-2022**).

"We need to turn back on the gas spicket. The Biden Administration has caused a large chunk of this inflation its primarily energy based..."(**Dave Ramsey** on **One Nation with Brian Kilmeade**, April 23rd, 2022).

White House advisor Brian Deese claims high gas prices are necessary for the future of the 'liberal world order'. (**White House advisor claims high prices necessary for 'future of the liberal world order', Just the News** article by: **Ben Whedon,** Updated July 2nd, 2022, 7:00 AM).

"You can't control the Environment; you'll find things like fossils on the top of the Grand Canyon..." (**Katie Pavlich** on **The Five**, November 6th, 2021).

"What is it about that (Marx) philosophy that has been so enduring? When it constantly promises Heaven, but delivers Hell?" (**Pete Hegseth** on **Life, Liberty, and Levine,** July 18th, 2021).

"And if you live in a poor inner city where there are no goods and high crime you don't care what the weather will be in 50 years, 'climate change' is the greatest white privilege in the world." (**Jimmy Failla** on **Gutfeld!** June 28th, 2022).

*"The council said that according to its latest figures, Nicolás Maduro won the election **by 1.49** percentage points, or fewer than 225,000 votes."* (**Venezuela election final results show narrower victory for Nicolás Maduro- Belle News- Read Think Share**).

"Freedom is a fragile thing and it's never more than one generation away from extinction…" (**Ronald Reagan**) (January 5th, 1967, 1st Public Inaugural Address as Governor of Ca-Ronald Reagan Presidential Library and Museum-**reaganlibrary.gov**).

"**Meet the new Squad: AOC poses alongside group members at opening of Congress**- Independent- **Namita Singh** -Monday 4th of January 2021- **independent.co.uk**).

"What do Republicans stand for?" -**President Biden** – (January 19th, 2022, Press Conference).

"We stand for jobs; we stand for a strong economy…" (**Senator John Barrasso (R-Wy)** response to President Bidens's Question- on **America Reports with John Roberts and Sandra Smith**, January 20th, 2022).

"The Mainstream Media is the marketing branch of the Democratic Party" (**Jesse Waters** on **The Five**, 2020).

"Capitalism is not these big corporations. Capitalism is the small business owners…" (**Senator Marko Rubio (R-FL)** on **Hannity**, February 7th, 2022).

Why?

"Bernie Sanders is an authentic social justice warrior" and *"Radicalism is romantic"* (**Greg Gutfeld** on **The Five**, March 3rd, 2020).

(Chrysler and Howard Hughes). [This is where dreams are built and made, and futures are designed.] *"This is who we are as a country and every American benefits."* (**Tammy Bruce** on **The Next Revolution with Steve Hilton**, May 1st, 2022).

New York's 14th District represents more than 650,000 people across parts of the Bronx and Queens. (**Alexandria Ocasio Cortez Representing New Yorks 14th District**- Our District).

"After community backlash, Amazon has decided not to move forward with its plan to open a headquarters in Long Island City, Queens" (Hiroko Masuike/The New York Times-Photo credit- **New York Times** article: **Amazon Pulls out of Planned New York City Headquarters** By: **J. David Goodman, nytimes.com**, February 14th, 2019).

"Somewhere around 80% of Bronx residents receive some form of public assistance." (**Tommy Guttilla** lives in New York City- answer on **Which Is the Poorest Borough in New York City on Quora.com**).

"Between 1946 and 1991" (**What was the Cold War- National Geographic** by: **Erin Blakemore** Published March 22nd, 2019).

"They woke up one day I guess and decided that Marxism was right all along and that the Cold War should have never ended…" (**Senator Marko Rubio R-Fl** on **Hannity**, February 7th, 2022).

"They don't want children to have a mind of their own." (**Albert R. Schneider,** January 2022).

"Because socialism is not about economics, It's about power…" (**Senator Marko Rubio R-Fl** on **Hannity**, February 7th, 2022).

"Mindless and casual labeling: racist/sexist/hater/xenophobic to stop them from speaking." (**Amy Wax** Professor at Penn Law School- **Amy Wax on the Leftist Nightmare in Academia**- on **YouTube** - February 20th, 2018- 0n the **EDGARBRANDONSON.COM** website).

"Facebook and Twitter they are the 19th Century Robber Barrons." (**Victor Davis Hanson** on **The Story with Martha MacCallum**, April 14th, 2022).

"For democracy to survive, we need more content moderation, not less." (**Max Boot** -Washington Post Columnist - on **Twitter**, April 14th, 2022).

"Content moderation" it sounds really good, but it's a euphemism for censorship." (**Greg Gutfeld** on **The Five**, April 14th, 2022).

"I have a theory, at first, I thought that these people were all over reacting having this massive freakout over this small problem…" (**Kat Timpf** on **Gutfeld!** April 14th, 2022).

"Democrats want to control what is said and what is not said. That's why corporate America, social media is trying so hard to maintain their grip

on power to the point where entities like Twitter is doing what is averse to their shareholders interest to keep Elon Musk out" (**Kayleigh McEnaney** on **Jessie Watters Primetime**, April 21st. 2022).

"Ministry of Truth." "The Party told you to reject the evidence of your eyes and ears. It was their final, most essential command." (**George Orwell** in **1984**, copywrite 1949, 1977).

"All of a sudden now Liberals are saying they are afraid that people with different political views on the Left might get canceled on Twitter, voices might be silenced…" (**Sean Hannity** on **Hannity**, April 26th, 2022).

"Political opponents" (**Jesse Waters** on **Jessie Watters Primetime**, April 21st, 2022).

"The real danger that were facing as a society right now in this country is that this fundamental freedom guaranteed to every one of us as Americans, freedom of speech, is being threatened…"- (**Tulsi Gabbard** on **Tucker Carlson Tonight**, February 2nd, 2022).

"We're all free spirits!" - (**Curtis Sliwa** on **Gutfeld!** January 11th, 2022).

"And somehow those are endangered" (**Greg Gutfeld** on **Gutfeld!** January 11th, 2022).

"We have some really difficult challenges…"- (**Governor Ron Desantis**- on **Life, Liberty and Levin**, January 9th, 2022).

"What is going on with society… (**Ari Fleischer** on **Gutfeld!** January 25th, 2022).

"Weak people are for censorship…" (**Tucker Carlson** on **Tucker Carlson Tonight**, February 2nd, 2022).

Conditions in jails in DC and VA, that are suffering from*: "denial of medical care, physical abuse, sleep disruption, verbal intimidation threats, denial of religious practices."* (**Suzanne Monk**-May 10th, 2022).

"(71 out of 725) while the other nine-tenths people are just being left there to rot, some are being sentenced to up to 5 years in prison" (Information gathered by**: Nik Popli** and **Julia Zorthian** at **TIME.com**, January 6th, 2022).

Aunt Kitty's Journey:

Perot believed Americans were disillusioned with the state of politics as being corrupt and unable to deal with vital issues. (Wikipedia, 2022).

"[Make no mistake about it] the Obamas were the creators and starting point of all the division and current anti-American chaos we're witnessing in America today." (**Joanie M. Lomax** on **Facebook**, December 23rd, 2019).

"Drain the Swamp!" - (**President Donald Trump** from 2016 and following 4 years…).

"Vocational Schools, and Apprenticeship Programs" (**Mike Rowe** on **Gutfeld!** May 2nd, 2022).

"Forgiveness of college loans is a handout to the rich." (**Sean Duffy** on **The Five**, June 10th, 2022).

"The American economy is experiencing the highest inflation rate in 40 years since 1982" (**Bret Baier** on **Special Report**, January 12th, 2022).

Build Back Better agenda with social and climate change policy which is riddled with handouts for special interest groups who want a piece of the pie. ('**Build Back Better is more about handouts than Human Infrastructure**', A Free Market Economy, **Students for Liberty**, article by: **Russel Coates**, published on December 10th, 2021).

That year 1.7 million people crossed illegally, and that number is estimated to go up to 2.1 million people by the end of the 2022 Fiscal year according to Princeton Policy Advisors. (**Even more illegal migrants expected in 2022, record 2.1 million, Washington Examiner**, by: **Paul Bedard**, April 19th, 2022, **washingtonexaminer.com**).

Biden's DOJ (Department of Justice) is suing Arizona over "proof of citizenship voter law" (**American Reports**, July 6th, 2022) [That is how desperate they are becoming] (**Sandra Smith** on **America Reports**, July 6th, 2022) [According to the UN: "the US Southern Border is the deadliest in world]. (Pete Hegseth, **America Reports**, July 6th, 2022).

"There is no statutory ability for the city of New York to issue inconsistent laws permitting non-citizens to vote and exceed the authority granted to it by the New York State Constitution." (Justice Ralph J. Porzio) ('**New York City's Noncitizen Voting Law is Struck Down**', The New York Times, article by: **Jeffery C. Mays**, June 27th, 2022).

"The liberal leaders are governing cities where hard working Americans taxpayers do not want to live in a dangerous, violent, filthy, expensive hell hole whether it is San Francisco or New York." (**Dagen McDowell** on **The Five**, June 10th, 2022).

"76% of New Yorkers are in fear that they will be a victim of violent crime." (**Will Cain** on **The Five**, June 10th, 2022).

June 30th, 2022 was the deadline to get the vaccine for the Military, and 40,000 US Service men and women chose not to get the vaccine, which is 13%. Now the government does not know what to do with them, this mandate is grounds for termination. (**Laura Ingraham on The Ingraham Angle**, July 5th, 2022).

"Kids don't see color, why force them to?" (**Frederick Douglas**) (**Brian Kilmeade** on **One Nation with Brian Kilmeade**, February 5th, 2022).

"Critical race Theory is nothing more than state sanctioned racism" (**Vice President Mike Pence** on Tuesday, April 12th, 2022).

"Even though we face the difficulties of today and tomorrow…" (-**Martin Luther King, Jr "I have a Dream"** speech- Lincoln Memorial on August 28th, 1963. *Copyright © 2010 NPR).*

"Within 30 days of receiving funds, develop and publish plans to safely reopen schools for in-person instruction." (Public Law No: 117-2 (March 11th, 2021) (**American Rescue Plan Act of 2021- Congress.gov**).

[Americans are] "frustrated, disappointed, nervous" (CBS News Poll January 12-14, 2022).

"They are the Democratic Socialist Party". (**Jeff Van Drew** on **One Nation with Brian Kilmeade**, February 5th, 2022).

The Difference Between Social Democracy in Europe and Socialism rearing its head in USA:

(5 trillion) "President Joe Biden will propose $5 trillion in new federal spending over the next decade on Friday as part of his fiscal year 2022 budget request." (**CNBC -Bidens Budget will include 5 trillion in new government spending over the next decade** by: **Christina Wilkie and Ylon Mui**- Published: Thursday May 7th, 2021).

"We are all paying back the free stimulus money now with inflation through the roof. This is the price we pay for free money. Nothing is free." (**Nelwyn Birch** on **Facebook**, February 18th, 2022).

Infrastructure Investment and Jobs Act- 11/15/2021- Public Law No: 117-58 (for 1.85 Trillian dollars) passed. (H.R. 3684- Infrastructure Investment and Jobs Act, **Congress.gov, 117th Congress 2021-2022**).

"The obvious reason for inflation is because the government printed a zillion amount more money than it had. It's very basic, not super-complicated. Like in Venezuela, the poor people of Venezuela have been run roughshod by their government." (tape of: **Elon Musk** on **The Faulkner Focus,** May17th, 2022).

"When you put more money in the economy, you devalue the dollar and its worthless." (**Sean Duffy** on **The Faulkner Focus**, May 17th, 2022).

"We know half a trillion was stolen of PPE(P) for businesses..." (on **Gutfeld!** March 31st, 2022).

"This administration has made it very clear that the Green New Deal and Climate Change and billions of dollars running through DC is their agenda..." (**Stephanie Nash** on **Tucker Carlson Tonight**, April 25th, 2022).

CARES ACT of 2020 (1.9 trillion)- (**Committee for a Responsible Federal Budget- Breaking Down 3.4 trillion in Covid Relief** -January 7th, 2021).

American Rescue Plan Act of 2021 (1.9 trillion) -(bipc.com-**Buchanan Ingersoll Rooney- Analysis: Congress Passes 1.9 trillion Covid-19 Relief Package**, March 10th, 2021).

(**SmartAssets- The House Passes the 1.85 trillion Dollar Build Back Better Act- Here's What's in It**- By: **Arturo Cond**e, **smartasset.com**, January 8, 2022,).

"From the time Biden's American Rescue Plan passed to today, inflation has *consistently run ahead of wages and delivering a substantial pay cut to all Americans, and everybody knows it."* (**Dana Perino** on **The Five**, March 30th, 2022).

"The UK's National Health Service does NOT ban private health insurance. Sweden has massive school choice and vouchers. Denmark has one of the lowest levels of government regulations in world." (**Steve Hilton** on **The Next Revolution**, February 23rd, 2020).

*"**Legos** and **IKEA** are not brought to you by socialism, it is the FREE MARKET that makes that available to you"* (**Kristen Soltis Anderson**-on the **Greg Gutfeld Show**, February 29th, 2020).

"Since he was elected Mayor of Burlington, Vermont in 1981"- "The Bulk of His Wealth Come from Book Deals and Sales" (**Town and Country- How Bernie Sanders Became a Millionaire**).

"Today I am making it clear to protect our Democracy I support..." (**Joe Biden's** speech in **Georgia**, January 11th, 2022).

"Fundamentally changing the Institution [of the Senate]." (**Mitch McConnell (R-Ky)** on **Special Report with Bret Baier**, January 20th, 2022).

"Mules"- (**2000 Mules- Documentary Film** by **Dinesh D'Souza - for sale on AMAZON**).

"That was an election un-like any we have experienced in our history." (**Molly Hemingway** on **The Faulkner Focus**, July 1st, 2022).

"If a political party does not have the foundation in the determination to advance a cause that is right..." (**Dwight D. Eisenhower**).

"He [President Biden] adopted the Bernie Sanders prescription for America..." (**Mitch McConnell (R-Ky)** [Senate Minority Leader] on **Special Report with Bret Baier**, January 20th, 2020).

"I don't know why the activists are so upset about Joe..." (**Greg Gutfeld** on **The Five**, January 11th, 2022).

"The Constitution sets out the power of the Federal Government..." (**Trey Gowdy** on **Sunday Night in America**, January 31st, 2022).

"The House and the Senate, and the Judiciary and the Executive branches work together to balance each other out, it's called a "Checks and Balances" system." (**Pat Templeton**, January 20th, 2022).

Democratic Socialism vs Socialism, Failed Socialist Countries, Successful Socialist Countries, Democratic Socialist Countries Populations, Finland's Review- (**Worldpopulationreview.com**).

"Under President Roosevelt, Social Security established a promise that lasts to this day: "growing old would never again mean growing poor" (**OUR HISTORY- democrats.org**).

Three Countries that tried Socialism and Rejected it: -Israel, India, and the United Kingdom... as British Prime Minister said: Margaret Thatcher — *"The problem with **socialism** is that you eventually run out of other people's money."*(**The Heritage Foundation- Written by Lee Edwards Ph. D**, Oct 16th, 2019).

The Crisis Situation:

Democrats: *"Let no crisis go to waste"* (**Laura Ingraham** on **The Ingraham Angle**, March 12th, 2020).

"It is better to reign in Hell than to serve in Heaven" (Fox News Contributor).

"You cannot expect the Government to do everything for you...at some point you have to take care of yourself" (**Dana Perino** in reference to the Coronavirus on **The Five**, March 6th, 2020).

"They [Socialists] are not creative, just controlling" [talking about Coronavirus,] *they have not discovered the cure, but will take credit and use that to their advantage..."* (**Greg Gutfeld** on **The Five**, March 9th, 2020).

"The thing about the Pandemic is..." (**Robert Smith** on **Cavuto Coast to Coast**, January 26th, 2022).

"The Democrats are expert practitioners of the politics of fear" (**Dinesh D'Souza** on **The Ingraham Angle**, May 12th, 2020).

"Democrats are relying on the vulnerability that they create to enact their agenda. Injecting fear and panic to push this multi trillion-dollar disaster." (**Dinesh D'Souza** on **The Ingraham Angle**, 5-12-20).

"The world is going to end in 12 years if we don't address climate change" (**Alexandria Ocasio-Cortez**, January 22nd, 2019).

"I think this green approach to governing is a religion for the Democratic Party..." (**Fred Fleitz** on **Fox News Live**, February 25th, 2022).

"This study focused on voting... (**Emily Compagno** on **Gutfeld!** 1-11-22 in reference to a study out of New York University: "**American society becoming more liberal than 50 years ago but voting for more republicans" Released Monday**, (January 10th, 2022).

Culturally Speaking

Core beliefs of Democrats and Republicans between the 1970's – 2010's (Discussion between **Gary Gerstle** and **E.J. Dionne** at **Politics and Prose**, Washington DC, April 20th, 2022).

"These two power brokers worked together on legislation that would shape America's political economy for a generation." (**Gary Gerstle, "The Rise**

and Fall of the NeoLiberal Order: America and the World in the Free Market Era", published by Oxford University Press, 2022, p 15).

"I have never been so discriminated against until I came out as a Republican." (**Madeleine Templeton**: Aunt Kitty, June 14th, 2022).

Washington Commanders Head Coach Ron Riviera fines Defensive Coordinator 100,000$ over a tweet. (**Gutfeld!** 6-14-22 -Commanders' Ron Riviera on DC Jack Del Rio's 100K fine: 'This is about him impacting the team' by Kevin Patra, **NFL.com**, June 14th, 2022).

"Seems to be that they pick lousy stances based on what we choose. If I decide I'm going to come out in favor of breathing, the democrats are going to say you know what- they are just going to stop breathing, and it's a weird petulant way to choose the things you believe in." (**Greg Gutfeld** on **The Five**, April 29th, 2022).

What really is Marxism? According to Whitaker Chambers it is: *"The 2nd oldest religion known to man founded by the serpent who whispered to Eve "ye shall be as gods." It's a profound human force, a profound desire to believe that you know good and evil, and then to seek to define good and evil for others."* (**Max Eden-** on **The War on the West**, May 5th, 2022).

"Whoever says he is in the light, yet hates his brother, is still in the darkness." (1 John 2:7-10, from: **Give Us This Day -AELred Senna**, OSB Publisher, 2022 -Evening of April 27th, 2022, 375).

"You're also seeing a generational change where Republicans are finally growing up, growing some courage and fighting back…" (**J.D. Vance** on **Unfiltered with Dan Bongino**, April 23rd, 2022).

"Latinos are soundly rejecting the Democratic Party since 2012 -2020. The Latina vote for Democrats is down 8%, and up 8% for Republicans. That's 16% more toward Republicans in the Latino Community." (**Steve Hilton** on **The Next Revolution with Steve Hilton**, April 24th, 2022).

"I don't think the Democratic Party is really listening. They have gone so far left that basically we, Latinos, don't recognize the party anymore…" (**Gloria Romero** on **The Next Revolution with Steve Hilton**, April 24th, 2022).

Voice of Sergio Gomez, Restaurateur-
(Sergio Gomez, Interview on April 26th, 2022).

"You need laws. Executive Orders come and go… (**Geraldo Rivera** on **The Five**, April 26th, 2022).

"African Americans approve of President Biden 67% down from 20 point. Those words resonate and what Donald Trump was saying, there is an element of truth…" (**Herald Ford, Jr.** on **The Five**, April 29th, 2022).

"After summer of 2020 we'd heard that Black Lives Matter took in, I think, 90 million Dollars…" (**Leo Terrell** on **Fox and Friends**, April 5th, 2022).

"Anyone that is surprised by BLM's shady shenanigans haven't been paying attention…" (**Shemeka Michelle** on **One Nation with Brian Kilmeade**, April 9th, 2022).

"This is so very very sad because so many people believe in the Black Lives Matter, the Movement, it was the organization…" (**Judge Jeanine Pirro** on **The Five**, April 5th, 2022).

"Black Lives Matter was a pseudo radical movement that exploited the suffering, and the irony is that it did nothing to save black lives..." (**Reverend Eugene Rivers III** on **Cross Country with Lawrence Jones**, April 24th, 2022).

Voice of a Black Woman, Sierra: (Interview on February 27th, 2022).

Voice of a Black Man, Malcolm: (Interview on April 30th, 2022).

"Deaths of police officers has gone up from 46 in 2020 to 73 in 2021. That is a 56% increase." (On- **The Five**, April 26th, 2022).

"Violence against law enforcement in this country is one of the biggest phenomenon's that doesn't get enough attention…" (**Christopher Wray** [FBI Director] on **The Five**, April 26th, 2022).

Voice of a Native American, Savannah: (Savannah, Interview on May 4th, 2022).

Voice of an Immigrant, Funmilay Ogunbiya: (Funmi, Interview on May 5th, 2022).

Voice of a Transgender Woman: (A.S.) (A.S., Interview on May 3rd, 2022).

Log Cabin Republican's History: (Logcabin.org).

"There are over 80 chapters nationwide." (**Jose E. V. Cunningham**, May 18th, 2022).

"Despite all the drama, we all have a purpose to support a cause that is bigger than ourselves." (**Al Wexler**, April 26th, 2022).

Voice of a Gay Man, Adam Savit: (Adam Savit, President of Log Cabin Republicans, DC Chapter, Interview on May 1st, 2022).

"Conservatism, in the classical sense, signifies respect for tradition, deference to existing institutions and the hierarchies that structure them, and are suspicious of change." (**Gary Gerstle, "The Rise and Fall of the Neoliberal Order: America and the World in the Free Market Era"**, published by Oxford University Press, 2022, p 4).

"The coming apart of the neoliberal order opened up space for Trump- style authoritarianism and Sanders- style socialism to flourish." (**Gary Gerstle, "The Rise and Fall of the Neoliberal Order: America and the World in the Free Market Era"**, published by Oxford University Press, 2022, p 3).

"We cannot move forward to a post-carbon world without a shift to a socialist system." (**Climate Solutions: Beyond Capitalism, by Tina Landis**, Liberation Media: San Fransisco, 2020, p 55).

The Dutch government is actively trying to seize farmer's land for their globalist green vision to use for collective (state) land. The farmers are fighting back. (**Tucker Carlson on Tucker Carlson Tonight**, July 7th, 2022).

China is the world's worst polluter and leads in CO2 emissions by over 50%. (**Worldometer**: CO2 Emissions by Country: China - 29.18%, United States – 14.02%, 2016).

"The credo here is 'Big Government Socialism', they want to transform the economy away from the principles of Free Market Capitalism…" (**Larry Kudlow** on **Life, Liberty, and Levine**, July17[th], 2022).

In Conclusion:

"You have a freer life if you are a Capitalist!" (**Greg Gutfeld** on **Gutfeld!** January 11th, 2022).

"False promises of Utopia's" (**Charlie Kirk** (Students for Trump) on **Life Liberty and Levine**, March 1st, 2020).

"It's time to embrace capitalism, not to abandon the values that make America the envy of the world" **Nikki Haley (US Ambassador to UN) -Wall Street Journal: "This Is No Time to Go Wobbly on Capitalism,"** article: Thursday, February 27th, 2020).

"There is no Unity, Jow Biden doesn't want Unity. What Joe Biden wants is for every American to bend the knee to his agenda". (**Representative Byron Donalds** on **American Reports with Sandra Smith and John Roberts**, September 6th, 2022).

About the Author

Madeleine "Kitty" Templeton graduated with a Bachelor of Arts degree in History from Dickinson College, Carlislie, Pa and has lived in the Washington DMV most of her life. Witnessing politics and protests in Estonia, the former Soviet Union, in 1990, and from extensive study of Russian History, Madeleine has gained a unique perspective on socialism and communism. In living in the Nation's capital, and from witnessing the national and local politics of Washington DC, Kitty has learned a thing or two about America. As the daughter of Pat Templeton, a conservative political consultant, growing up she has met several influential Republicans including Ronald Reagan, Bob Dole, and Tom Ridge and has finally come around to understand the conservative perspective and this philosophy and the true principles of standing up for your freedom, and the dangers of socialism creeping into America.

Kitty Templeton is also a Singer/Songwriter and Poet in the Washington DC community. You may find her books, music and poetry at her website: **AuntKittysCorner.com.** Stay tuned for Aunt Kitty's next Artistic creation!

To continue reading more about the creeping of Socialism in the United States:

Mark Levine's
"American Marxism"

Dinesh D'Souza's
"United States of Socialism"

George Orwell's
"1984" and "Animal Farm"